STANDING
ON THE
SIDE OF THE ROAD

The Story of a Young Boy Making a Decision
to Stop or Strive in Life

*The picture is the position of the writer standing where the boy
stood when he was denied the opportunity to get on a bus to
travel out of state with all the other children in his community.*

Clark Thomas

ISBN 979-8-88751-240-2 (paperback)
ISBN 979-8-88751-241-9 (digital)

Christian Faith Publishing
832 Park Avenue
Meadville, PA 16335
www.christianfaithpublishing.com

Printed in the United States of America

Preface

Many years have passed since I encountered my "standing on the side of the road" experience. I have attempted to write this book many times, but my thoughts were, *No one wants to read about the experience of a boy who came from a poor family living in a country place.* I never dreamed I would be where I am in life today: a pastor, receiver of national awards for my work in OSHA, with a beautiful family and much more.

Through the years, people who have heard about my story insisted that my story could help someone who is about to give up on life because they feel alone and see themselves as an outcast. I will admit, on several occasions, I considered suicide. Looking back, I realize all I would have missed if I had killed myself. Therefore, any parent, Sunday school teacher, schoolteacher, youth leader, pastor, or a child who reads this book can use my story as an example to tell someone similar to how I was, about a person who was at rock bottom as a youth and, instead of giving up, fought his way through seemingly hopeless situations and became a successful person who aided many others to have a good life.

I want everyone to know that my life's journey made me who and what I am, which is to help somebody along life's way. The pictures and letters from individuals will help you see how the Lord will and can use people who think they have nothing to offer.

Finally, I have a skit I wrote a long time ago about the danger of putting off. This skit hopefully will encourage someone who wants to change their life to come to know that procrastinating is an enemy to change and become a productive, happier person.

As you read this book, I bet you will see yourself or someone you may know or have known in my story.

Acknowledgments

I want to give thanks to the many people who pushed me for many years to put this story in writing. Many of the people said my story would help so many other youths who have been left behind, who'd given up. They would be able to see that success is in the hand of the person who doesn't give up but strives to do better.

Additionally, I thank my wife, Hazel Boyd Thomas, who pushes me to never give up regardless how dim the outcome looks and who is always in prayer for me.

My daughter, Vaccarlo Cartez Thomas Allen, who died from COVID, believed I could do anything and did so much of my typing.

My sons Patrick Ezell Thomas and Ivan Clark Thomas, who have always been so much joy in my life, who also believed in me.

My oldest grandsons, Kelsey Thomas and Freddie Culclager, have been in my life since birth, and they have always looked up to me. My oldest granddaughter, Kieona Culclager, who is a big part of my heart, was the one who tackled and read my writing and typed the drafts.

Finally, I thank my nephew, Dr. Rev. Larry Holmes, who encouraged me to finish writing my little book a few months before he died. I owe him so much.

Lastly, all the members at New Salem Church, who have been in so many of the plays I wrote and traveled on the many trips we took. Also the ones who wrote letters and provided pictures for this book. I know there are others I left out. I thank them also.

Introduction

I write this book years later after facing pains, hurts, and feeling isolated for my age level. I hope this book will encourage all who felt as an outsider and always looked over.

I was thirteen years old when I faced one of the deepest frustrations to confront a young boy who was born and raised in a lower-class family living in a sharecropper's house at the mercy of a white boss. He made sure his field was worked by farmers who had children. Early on in life, I dealt with an inferiority complex.

Because of this early background and how we had lived, it created negative self-worth that resulted in low self-esteem. At the tender age of thirteen, when I should have been enjoying a new era, I was given a blow that made me feel (1) rejected, (2) alone, and (3) even more isolated from my peers, who seemed to have it all together. As for me, I felt like crap.

There was an event where one person decided to not let me get on a bus going to Louisiana, which caused crappy feelings to come over me and lingered for years. It finally motivated me to write this book. After what happened that day, I actually found myself standing on the side of the road in Tucker, Arkansas, alone, crying, and not knowing what to do other than feel like a loser.

While standing on the side of the road alone, crying, and lost, I was facing a defining moment in my life that could impact my future forever. I had to decide, Would I give up on life and permit this to make me feel alone standing on the side of the road, pouting every time I am faced with any challenge? Or would I fight and become an overcomer?

This book aims to help anyone who may want to give up when they feel left out and alone. I hope by reading this book, individuals will find strength to fight. This book is to help anyone believe you can eventually become a champion over all challenges you might face. After reading this book, my hope is, you will come to realize that quitting is not an option.

As an individual who stood on the side of the road, this is not easy for a young boy or girl. I can attest there were storms that stalks within me, causing psychological and emotional damage that took years to repair. I will share with readers how standing on the side of the road led me to make many choices that were difference-makers for me. Also, how the "standing on the side of the road" moment became a motivator instead of a demotivator in approaching life.

Readers will realize that no matter what you think or what you may go through, you are still in control of your purpose in life and how you respond to each event. Though each event is hidden until you come face-to-face with the challenges, you can't quit. You must push on, no matter how often the letdowns come.

The big question every individual will face is, Will they give up and drown in self-pity alone, or will they fight to be an overcomer and be a good example to those straddling the fence, trying to decide whether to quit or fight on?

Finally, I want the readers to realize that no one should ever try to walk this journey alone because standing on the side of the road creates indescribable hurts, pains, frustrations, anger, etc. that seemingly will never go away. These hurts can become strength destoyers, if you don't have an encourager to walk beside you.

Where My "Standing on the Side of the Road" Experiences Began—With My Family

I decided to write some history about how little things in your early childhood can play a role in how one handles things when you get older. My inner troubling feelings started long before I was thirteen. The thirteen-year-old event is what brought out the things I had hidden within my subconscious. Therefore, I first want to introduce you where my difficult life seems to have begun and brought on my lonely feelings. After my reflecting on my early days, I will call my early-age experience, where I stood on the side of the road prior to the age of thirteen. This will help readers understand why standing on the side of the road at the age of thirteen and the experiences beyond that were crushing.

Therefore, my "standing on the side of the road" experiences began after I perceived how I fitted in with my family and people around me. This is where my self-inflicted feelings started. My early problems were not labeled as standing on the side of the road until I understood the day I actually stood on the side of the road alone and hurt. Standing on the side of the road is a result of being alone and hurt.

My family consisted of individuals who had good talents and an impressive makeup. It was my thoughts about who I was and what I lacked when I compared all the good things my siblings had going for them that caused my problem. I felt that I came up short in all categories in the gifts and talents my siblings had. This made me feel much lesser than my brothers and sisters. Therefore, my self-esteem took a beating because of my lack of achievements, especially when I saw my siblings overachieve. The mistake I made early was, I wanted to be someone else so I could be somebody. I thought God had done me wrong. I concluded that nothing about me was not as good as my siblings'. Therefore, when it came to my ability to do little things like singing, sports, and education (I even had a problem riding a bike), they were always great, but I fell short compared to them. I hoped that people could see that my self-esteem was weak or, for lack of a better word, on life support; and they would say or do something to make me feel better.

Something as Small as Picking Berries Created a Problem for Me

Picking blackberries was normal for us to do every summer. All youth in our little community picked berries. We picked berries so my mother could can them for the winter to cook berry pies and berry dumplings. If I had not said it previously, I'll say it again: my family was poor.

At the close of the day, the disappointment would come when we returned home with our buckets of berries. Momma would look at my brother's bucket of berries and then my bucket. Many times she would lovingly say to me, "You have too many red berries. I really can't use those." Then she would take a look at my older brother's bucket and proceed to pour his berries into the dish pan and start to prepare them for canning.

I was left with unusable red berries. My spirit went down, but I would hold my feelings to myself. On the other hand, my brother felt proud. It wasn't a sibling rivalry. It was a little boy who didn't understand, and no one took time to notice he needed help.

What happened afterward, which is another event that stood out to me, was that my brother came and asked me to come go play. It never occurred to him I was hurting; he didn't consider my pains. May I add, my brother loved me, and my mother meant no harm. Regardless, within me, all I could feel was that I could never measure up even when it came to picking berries. *They say little foxes kill the vine. According to Song of Songs 2:15, I can basically say that little hurts can ruin a child.*

1

A child has to face a number of things. Some things seem like nothing to older people like this next encounter I had. It was one summer which was cotton-chopping time. I was this child that people looked down upon. I wanted to go with my brother to the cotton field, but everyone said I was too little. I was the baby of the family. The last child no one understood. This small rejection caused me to feel alone, like an outcast. Everyone else saw no harm in this because they were not me. This type of misunderstanding can happen in any family when someone doesn't take time to try and walk in a hurting child's shoes.

Little did they know, I was hurting because I was losing what was precious to me: being part of the group. I just wanted to belong and be affirmed. I wanted my friends to believe I was just as good as everyone else. Because I was not included, I felt like an outcast. It drove me deeper into loneliness, and loneliness is painful.

Therefore, at this stage in my life, I started to build up anger and self-pity. My anger was not directed at my family and friends. I was just becoming an angry boy who wanted to fight at the drop of a hat. This was my survival mechanism. I couldn't explain what was happening. I just had a quick temper and was out of control.

Everything I just shared with you took place on top of what happened to me when we lived in Sherrill, Pastoria, Arkansas.

While living Pastoria, I remember I couldn't ride a bike, but my brothers could. I took it upon myself to force my way on the bicycle with others. When I did, I overloaded the bike, and it turned over in a curve in the road, and we were nearly ran over. It didn't bother me because I felt neglected. We once lived right next to Horseshoe Lake where everyone fished. My mama wouldn't let me bait my hook because I didn't know how to even bait a hook; she could have at least permitted me to try and not shame me in front of other people. I believe a child should have a chance to fail.

Let me share a story of how my feelings at a very early age caused me to act violently. I was an elementary student at Sherrill Rosenwald school. This was where I went for bad (this was the way I tried to belong). There was another boy whom everyone bragged about being tough. I felt that if he was the one everyone bragged about, where would that leave me? (Yes, standing on the side of the road as a nobody). I was feeling like a nobody, in my family and everywhere else.

Because of my low feeling about myself, it drove me to take matters into my hands. I took steps, to feed my low feelings, and built myself up. There was a boy at my elementary school the children bragged about who rode the same bus I did. When we started to get off the bus, I hit him behind the head, but that was the only blow I got in. The only little good that came out of this was, that boy and I became good friends. He dared anyone to say anything about me or to me.

However, this still put me in second place. That's not good, but the whooping kept me silent.

Why did I add this story? When negatives build up in a child and he or she talks to themselves and then answers themselves, bad actions will follow. When you tell yourself negative things and then agree with those negatives, bad things will result. Even when my intent was to reduce the accumulation of more pain, I only added more pain in my life. Later on that year, I looked into the mirror and saw everything that I had tried to cover up: a sad, out-of-control kid.

Will a new location help? Changing locations will only change the scenery, not your inner self.

In 1956, my family moved to Tucker, Arkansas. This is the place where the thought "standing on the side of the road" really got its start. I was a little older now in a new location. I felt my change would come. That day, a new location, new people, new this, new that—everything was just new. I quickly found out no matter where you move, the greatest enemy to self-perception and change is the self. My problem was that I was a child and didn't know about tact and adjustments. This is what I learned: whenever you move, you carry yourself with you. You carry your looks, abilities, or lack thereof with you. You also carry unhealed hurt everywhere you go.

There is one good thing about relocating, if there is one at all. Since I was an outsider and no one knew me, I thought this was a plus. But the danger for me was, my desires for newness that I thought would automatically make things better became my blind spot to reality. Since I was new, I wanted to be impressive and make a name for myself. Therefore, I made a big mistake by doing one crazy thing. I tried to replace the drum major of the community, the person who was my age whom the school and community had already accepted as the one person who had proven himself.

A lesson all young people should learn when you move to a new location is, never try to take the place of the person who have been embraced by the people. The same year, 1956, I wore blinders that caused me to weigh the option of whether an outsider could unseat a person who lived in the community. I made a choice to try and bulldozer my way into the spotlight so I could not only be accepted but be the leader. *One thing any outsider must do that I never considered before trying to be a leader is, you must first be accepted, then be assimilated. All the people saw was a self-centered outside boy trying to take over.*

On the other hand, my brothers were readily accepted. I mean quickly. I concluded, *Here it goes again. I am about to find myself alone, hurting, and no one cares.*

After a few days and months, new pains and hurts started to accrue upon the old ones. It wasn't long before these hurts and pains created an even lower self-esteem in me. My deep hurts on top of rejection in the new location, it started me to believe this was the way my life would always be. Therefore, I thought about hurting myself. I thought this would make people show they care. I just wanted attention. I guess I was too much of a coward to hurt myself.

One of the things everyone failed to do was to take time to consider my behaviors. In everyone else's eyes, I was a person who didn't measure up, and this was how I believed they were thinking.

A Word to Parents

Parents, when your children seem normal, remember they all have issues, no matter how loving a family maybe. Never assume your child is free from their inner battles caused by Satan. Every child will have a crack in their emotional armor. Parents, always have an open spirit where your child or children would feel motivated to talk to you. *Only by having someone to talk to will a hurting child be able to lighten their load.*

My First Possible Breakthrough

In the fifth grade, my teacher left me in charge of the class to take names of anyone out of order. I was my teacher's errand boy who carried messages to other teachers. This made me feel good. In fact, teachers sent positive messages home to my parents. The teacher told my mother I had good leadership skills, and I would make a difference one day. To have something good said about me made me feel good.

This possible breakthrough was short-lived because my fellow playmates said I was a teacher's pet. They looked at me as someone not good to be around because I was a snitch. I had to make a choice not with what was right or wrong but what would make me popular with peers. I knew I couldn't run with the old folks; I started showing my peers they didn't have anything to worry about.

I learned a valuable lesson: you can't please two different groups, and I lost favor with the teacher. One teacher sent word to my mother, who was the president of the PTA, about my behavior. My mother and teachers were highly disappointed in me. After all that happened, it appeared everyone was out to get me. When everything was over, the young people still followed the person who always was the favorite in the school. Once again, I was on the outside.

Second Positive Breakthrough That Didn't Last Long

Later on, in the seventh grade, I made the softball team and became the starting short stopper. Well, I would have made the team anyway because at my school, we only had enough people to make up a team. Nevertheless, I was on the team, starting. I was now in the spotlight.

My chance to shine finally happened. A ground ball was hit to me. I picked it up and started a double play. The kids called my name. The principal and coach bragged on me. I said to myself, *Now I belong.* For the next few weeks, I received pats on the back and so many encouraging words.

Every day I wanted things to change for me. It did; another breakthrough happened. I was chosen to play a major role in a play entitled *Where's That Report Card?* I played the role as Junior. In the play, Junior always went to the mailbox to get the mail. He was trying to beat his parents to the mailbox because he knew he had bad grades. The report cards finally came in the mail, and as expected, Junior had very bad grades. Junior decided to hide the report card because if he had bad grades, he would be punished and not able to go play outside for weeks at a time. It was a good play, and the people of the community really bragged about my good acting.

Everyone else had gotten their report card. Junior's parents started inquiring one day as he was trying to hide the card. He backed into the tea kettle and burned his behind and dropped the card. At the end, he was punished. The play was a success.

By this time, I was riding on cloud nine. My advice to anyone who is riding high: take a note from what I learned—a great ups and downs always come; some sooner than later. For me, my down came sooner. Nothing remains the same. Most of the time the direction is down.

Dip After the Rise

This is where, at age thirteen, my true experience for standing on the side of the road took place.

Another year passed, and I was promoted to the eighth grade. What a difference a year makes. I had two triumphs, and people bragged on me. They bragged about my performance in the dramatic play and how I turned the double play on the softball field. After these victories, I faced one of the greatest hurts that happened in my life. This hurt is the dip after I thought I had risen. This major hurt in my life was what motivated me to write this book. This is where the actual title of the book came about, *Standing on the Side of the Road*.

This dip in life felt like it created a free fall into my years of current existence. That free fall saw me standing on the side of the road alone. This occurrence pulled the scab off my old mental and emotional wounds. This challenged me to raise a red flag to warn others that old wounds never truly heal, and bad experiences only reopen those wounds that we believe have healed and are a thing of the past.

The experience I have shared so many times before I wrote this book did not just happen because of that particular day.

I came from a poor family of nine—children, mother, father, and a nephew. Many of us lived in the same house at one time or another. We didn't have running water; in fact, we had to use a pump to pump water and fill up a barrel and put lime in the water to cut the rust. The additional problem: we had to use an outdoor toilet. We just did not have much. Because of our economic problems, our opportunities were limited, and this played a role that caused me, at least that was my initial thought, to have to stand on the side of the road.

Because of my family's economic status, I did not travel across Arkansas. I had traveled seventeen miles to Pine Bluff, Arkansas, from where we lived. Maybe one time to Little Rock, Arkansas, which was about forty miles from where we lived in Tucker, Arkansas. *I learned this particular day the importance of traveling.*

A Lesson Learned

I learned several things: (1) the struggles and shame to have to stand on the side of the road with no one caring; (2) knowledge is blessed. Why didn't I know the answers to those questions? It was the result of not knowing the geography of the state of Arkansas. *This lack of knowledge about the state limited my ability to answer the questions I was asked about the state.*

My Hard-Core Story That Drove Me to Write This Book

I remember that day clearly and how I felt. It always feels like yesterday, even now at my age. I was a member of the 4H club. The club was going out of the state to give young students exposure. The trip was to Baton Rouge, Louisiana. Not only would I be going out the state for the first time in my life, I would be traveling on a trailway bus. This was one of my dreams, to travel on a trailway bus.

To be on that bus and go out of state would be the highlight of my life. All I had to do was answer a simple question. Well, I thought it was simple.

I played the thought in my mind. I'm going to finally get to travel out the state. My family wasn't able to afford trips, so this was a dream come true. Before I could qualify to board the bus, the sponsor said he had to ask me a question. The question was, "Name four rivers that are located in the state of Arkansas." The right answers meant I could get on the bus. Because I had not traveled to Arkansas and had not studied Arkansas geography, the only river I knew was the Arkansas River. I was able to guess upon the Black River and White River. The problem was, those were only three rivers; I was hoping those three would be enough.

There was a time period to answer the question. I sat there making every move, twitching, counting my fingers, making up river names in my head, trying to guess on the correct answer. It was evident to the sponsor that I didn't know the answer.

The sponsor looked at me and said, "I don't have all day." I twisted in my seat, rubbed my head, cleared my throat, and said, "All I know is three rivers." I begged him to let the three I knew be good enough. I really wanted to go. He waited awhile. He kept me in the hot seat. Then I heard him say, "I'm sorry, but you can't go." It wasn't the first time I had heard the word *no*. However, this time I thought since I knew the sponsor, he would change his mind.

I will interject this thought about the word *no*. I do know hearing *no* will help prepare you to hear *no* in the future. It is important for children to hear *no* sometimes to develop some tough skin. But the initial hearing of the word *no* that day was a little more than I could handle; it was hard.

The *no* answer that day didn't hurt as bad as what happened the next day. What happened the next day was like a stronghold choking on me. It seemed like I could not breathe.

This is what happened. That morning I got up. I packed my little bag knowing that the person who was in charge, who had eaten and slept at our home, would change his mind and let me go.

All the kids were there laughing, playing, etc. Plus the buses, the big trailway buses that I had never been on before were there. The children started running to line up at the door of the bus with extreme excitement. Everyone stood there with bright wide smiles, duffle bags, pillows, and blankets for the long road trip. Then the sponsor started to call the names of the ones that could board the bus. The first thirty names were called. Then the next seventeen names. The first bus was filled. The next bus pulled forward. The sponsor began calling more names, and as he called them, I hoped and believed mine would be next. But after he called the next forty-seven names, he turned and got on the bus with the other leaders.

This is where I stood hoping to get on the trailway bus.

Standing on the side of the road.

I walked away from where the buses were loaded and stood on the side of the road where the bus had to travel by. I stood at the side of the road and waited for the bus to ride by, hoping they would feel sorry for me and call my name to get on that bus.

Finally, the bus headed my way. I was holding my bag, so ready to get on that bus. Much to my surprise, the buses slowly passed me by. As the buses passed, the children waved at me. Someone even yelled out, "We'll be back."

This picture shows where I stood, pointing at
the direction the bus was traveling.

The buses went down the road. I ran and looked until the buses were out of sight. Then I felt alone, standing on the side of the road.

This picture show the direction the bus traveled to, out of my sight.

I looked around, and it dawned on me—I can't go. I'm left here all by myself. I was the only child my age left in Tucker.

My Reaction While Standing on the Side of the Road

This day was painful. I cried, and I cried, somewhat like David and his men did at Ziklag, as we read in 1 Samuel 30:1–5:

> David and his men reached Ziklag on the third day. Now the Amalekites had raided the Negev and Ziklag. They had attacked Ziklag and burned it, and had taken captive the women and everyone else in it, both young and old. They killed none of them, but carried them off as they went on their way.
>
> When David and his men reached Ziklag, they found it destroyed by fire and their wives and sons and daughters taken captive. So David and his men wept aloud until they had no strength left to weep. David's two wives had been captured—Ahinoam of Jezreel and Abigail, the widow of Nabal of Carmel.

I stood there crying, wishing and hoping the bus would return, but it did not. I even prayed, but that did not work either.

Finally, I started my long walk home holding my bag. The walk would be less than half a mile, but it seemed like I was many miles away. As I walked by houses in the community, I heard voices asking me, "Chunky, you didn't go? What happened to you? Did the bus leave you?"

I tried to act happy because I really did not want people to know I was too dumb to name four rivers in Arkansas. I started to blame everyone but myself. I felt God had let me down because I had prayed the night before. I believed God did not like me, just like everyone else.

The real task awaited me a few hundred feet away. How would I face my mother when I made it home? My mother came and asked what was wrong.

After a few minutes, tears began to fall, and my emotions became uncontrollable. I didn't have to say a word. My tears were all the answers she needed. All parents reading this book, if you have a child facing disappointments like me, do as my mother. She knew I did not need a fussing; I needed someone to show they cared. My mother hugged me and said, "One day you will go out of state on a bus just like that." I laid on my mother's shoulders. It helped a little, but I could not help but think about what my brother and friends were doing in Louisiana.

My Pains Turned Into a Plan

After a disappointing day, something amazing happened inside of me. It seemed like an epiphany. I made a discovery that night as I sat by myself at thirteen years old. I promised myself that if the Good Lord put me in a position to help prevent anyone from being like me when I found myself standing on the side of the road, I would do whatever it took to make sure no one experienced the smothering hurt and pain I felt on that disappointing, awful sunny day, when I had to stand and watch those trailway buses pass me by.

Later that night, I even made a deeper vow after crying a little more. I said I would help anyone with my finances, if I ever got any money, who felt left out just because they didn't measure up. Amazingly, once I made that vow, my throbbing pain eased up a little. I had vowed that one day I would make a difference. I really never thought it would happen or how all this would happen. I did not have a clue, but shifting my thoughts took away some of the pains. I did remain in the house the rest of the night.

Life seemed to have gotten better after I vowed to do things for others. My positive thinking appeared to be the key to feeling better. My life seemingly hit a period that night: *I will be okay because I am going to invest in someone else's life.* The trip is soon climaxed. Everyone returned home, and I was trying to put all that happened behind me and think about doing something new. Days passed. Everyone on the trip was reflecting on all that happened. I must admit, this hurt, but I couldn't show my pains. I kept thinking about what I had vowed to do.

Later On That Summer, a Breakthrough Came for Me

A young man decided to start a Little League baseball team, and the "standing on the side of the road" boy would become the starting pitcher. Me, Chunky, the one who could not name four rivers in Arkansas. I became starting pitcher.

This new found success made me feel like I was riding on a joyful bus in a new life. Success can help relieve bad memories.

When I pitched, people would call my name, cheering me on; and at this young age, it helped my ego. I felt this would be the way of life from now on. Little did I know another rough time awaited me. The time period that awaited me would make me feel like I was back standing on the side of the road. *Sometimes success is short-lived. I didn't realize it. I embraced the success, feeling as if it was permanent. It wasn't long. My "side of the road" experience happened again. Not with the ball, but it was my social life that put me back on the side of the road.*

It was one summer morning when a young man moved into our community from England, Arkansas. My experience about life became my downfall. I didn't know anything about courting; you know girls. Because I was dumb about this girl thing, I just thought when a girl said she was your girlfriend, she was just your girlfriend. Then things started to happen after this boy moved into the community. To start with, the boy's home was about one hundred yards from my girlfriend's house, and I was a long ways away. A few weeks later, I heard that my girl did not like me anymore. Day after day, I lived in a lake of worry; did she want me or him? I should have known something was going on; she was with him all the time. My life was once again started spinning out of control. After a few more days, I knew I had lost her to a stranger.

I wondered what she wanted with him. I started answering that question by thinking maybe because (a) he wore new clothes, (b) he was fairly good-looking, (c) he was a smooth talker, (d) he was an outsider with experience. I was just opposite of him. I didn't think that should make a difference, but it did make a big difference. The other girls were jealous of her; her man was walking around in starched and iron clothes, talking hot stuff. I didn't like him, but my girl did.

It wasn't long before I had to stand and watch them hold hands, laughing, playing, and looking at me out of the corner of their eyes. It was painful. The pain became more excruciating when the older boys made fun of me. To win some points, I tried to run him down. I said he can't even read, but one of the older boys who was dating his sister said, "He may not be able read, but he took your girl away from you." Again I was on the outside looking in. I just wanted to give up on life.

All I could say was, "Here it goes again, I'm standing on the side of the road, not watching a bus go by but watching another boy with my girl."

After many encounters, I decided not to go to the playground anymore. I did not want to be around anyone. Here I am again, alone, embarrassed, and hurt. I suffered for a period of time, but to my surprise, my recovery was not that difficult because my deepest hurt was when I stood on the side of the road watching the bus pass me by. As a song says, the first cut is the deepest. Therefore, this hurt was not as deep as the first hurt, where I actually stood on the side of the road and watched the buses go by carrying my friends out of state, but it still was a hurt that created many questions about myself. *I felt like Gideon in the Bible when he said these words about himself in Judges 6:14–15:*

> *The Lord turned to him and said go in the strength you have and save Israel out of Midian's hand. Am I not sending you. But Lord Gideon*

asked how can I save Israel? My clan is the weak-
est in Manasseh and I am the least in my family,
Actually this was the way I truly felt.

Deep within I wanted to be somebody who felt worthy of something. I thought if I was to become a leader, do great things, and change how I am viewed, I had to work on my self-esteem. After running these types of thoughts through my mind, I concluded, when you think like this, you are putting yourself at the bottom of the barrel because you start believing the only way to be somebody others have to approve you. *To be truthful, setbacks after setbacks will make you feel like a nobody and make you look for affirmation from anyone.*

Taking Another Shot at Making Myself Feel Important

Another stupid thing I did to make myself feel important took place when I was in the eighth grade.

Once again a teacher put me in charge of the class; this gave me a feeling of power. There was a young lady in the class who started to act up. I pulled off my belt and threatened to spank her. The teacher entered the classroom as I was pulling my belt out. What a tongue-lashing. Needless to say, I became the laughingstock of the classroom. I walked around all day with a bowed-down head; no one came to my rescue. *I learned never to try to elevate myself at the expense of others.*

The second thing I did to make myself feel important was later that spring. There was a school event, so I decided to do something for laughter. The school was filled with parents. I decided to lead a bunch of boys to do something exciting. We turned off the electrical main switch, so all the lights would go out. I thought it was funny; old folks were running in the hallway. Again instead of long-term satisfaction, the principal found out, and here it goes again. I got punished and had to pick up paper from all over the entire school-yard. Once again people were laughing at me. I was feeling alone. Evil actions never produce a good outcome.

After two tries at trying to make myself feel good and import-ant, I had one last bright idea. I convinced several boys to lie with me in a ditch and throw rocks at cars as they passed by. We hit this one car, the man stopped, and he had a spotlight on his car. He imme-diately shone it in our direction. He cussed, called us nigger boys, and said he was going to shoot us. We got away by hiding under the schoolhouse. Then we ran across the field to get away. We had great fear in our hearts. When it was over, I was blamed, and they were saying I could have gotten us killed. I was doing all of this trying to establish myself as a leader. Again I was looked down upon. I found myself once again all alone. After many years have passed, I can say, if I had known then what I know now, I wouldn't do such a dumb thing. *Most importantly, never blame yourself for the choices of others even if you suggest it.*

Afterward, all day at that school, I felt alone. Just as I did when I stood on the side of the road. I was abandoned by my so-called friends. Summer finally came, school was out, and the only thing we had to do for fun in Tucker was play baseball. At least I did good at that.

Somehow I Developed Resilience During the Summer

Something happened during that summer that caused me to recover from the hurt of losing my girlfriend. I started getting more deeply involved in summer activities such as baseball and makeup fun. Years passed, and I was still fighting my setbacks. The words of Job are true: "Man that is born of a woman is of few days and full of trouble." At church, I learned Jesus would be with you, that he would help me overcome any problem I faced or will face. I programmed myself to think I had a chance for a new start, one that I thought would make a difference.

A New Start After the Summer Was Over

The new start took place after summer when I passed to the ninth grade. My mother permitted my brother and me to attend another school. I knew this was my chance to prove that I was somebody. To begin with, there were so many girls at the new school, so I forgot all about my first girlfriend. I thought I was in girls' heaven.

Something I forgot: no matter where I go, I would always be the Chunky who stood on the side of the road; therefore, I had to change me.

My mother enrolled us at Altheimer High School, which later changed to Martin High, named after the principal Fred Martin Jr. The principal was my cousin. I thought this was the change that would give me a chance to become an overcomer, from bad to good. *There were great opportunities* At the new school, they had a gym, a cafeteria, and the food was hot. The school I previously went to, Tucker Rosenwald, had their meals brought in from another school in covered containers, which allowed room for the food to be tampered with. The school was about ten or twelve miles away. This was a predominately white segregated school *where our meals were prepared.* At their school, each grade had an independent classroom. At Tucker Rosenwald, there were two grades to a classroom. Altheimer High school offered much more; it had a legit basketball coach, library, science lab, separate rooms for each class, and a shop building where one could learn a trade. This school made me feel like I was on my way. When I went back to Tucker, I had my chest stuck out because I thought the new school would make me. I would later find out this wasn't so.

A few months after school started, it was basketball season. I decided to try out because I was a good basketball player, I thought. I soon realized that it would be a little different since I had only played basketball on the ground. The next thing that stood out at Tucker school was, there was only a handful of people going out for the team, so everyone was going to make it anyway. Finally, tryouts came at Altheimer High, and the gym was full of boys going out for the team, and the competition was stiff.

My excitement turned to feeling down after seeing those boys' ability. These guys were much better than the boys at Tucker. They were faster, jumped higher, knew how to run plays, understood the different types of passes and basketball terminology. I soon found out I had a long ways to go. However, I made the team. I did not play much during the season, but I had a position on the team. I got to sit and watch the game with my uniform on from the sidelines. You know this position on the team is the "bench warmer." I liked to look at myself as a "bench encourager" to my fellow teammates on the court. At least I had a basketball uniform, and I could go back to Tucker and brag.

The encouragement from the bench wasn't that bad. Then my pains came after each game. When the game was over, the players who played talked about how many points they scored. Many of them started making fun of me. They would turn to me and ask, "Chunk [that's my nickname], what did you do?" Another player would say, "All he did was pick splinters" (I sat on a wooden bench). I learned a valuable lesson. Situations and circumstances are created everywhere you go, and people can be coldhearted.

Once again, I found myself hurting. It seemed like hurting was a normal thing for me. Because of my past, the scars from standing on the side of the road reminded me I was alone once more. Before the season was over, I played some and even helped win a game against Star City. Boy, did it feel good to hear people cheering for me. I stole the ball and called a quick time-out. My coach said, "Great job, quick thinking," because the time would have expired if I had not called time-out. We won the game.

When the season ended, I was awarded a trophy. I was happy, elated, and started getting beside myself. I couldn't wait until my tenth grade year. I would be on the senior team with my brother, the Thomas boys from Tucker. I could see myself passing the ball to my big brother, like I did on the ground at Tucker, and he would score a bucket. My thoughts were out of this world.

Things don't always work according to plan. I did make the team, but that was about all the good that happened to me that year. My bad feelings started when I saw those other guys in practice. I knew then I would have another season of picking splinters. I knew I would never play unless it was a blowout. These were painful thoughts. Ever since my "side of the road" experience, when the buses passed me by, I learned you can't quit no matter how much it hurts and how the odds are against you. You may be laughed at, but quitting should never an option.

Throughout the season, I sat on the bench hoping and praying God would make the coach put me in, but my prayer turned out to be fruitless. There was a game I knew I would play in. The night of the game, my brother and I were late. We both had our basketball uniform in our hands as we ran into the gym. There were loud cheers from the stands. I smiled, but that was short-lived. They started calling my brother's name; it was as if I didn't exist. This was a bitter pill to swallow. The next pill was even worse.

When we went into the dressing room to put our uniforms on, they kept telling my brother to hurry up; none of the teammates called my name. I was feeling down, but I would feed myself positive thoughts to pick myself up. I said to myself, *This will be a blowout game. You will play tonight.* Furthermore, my siblings were in the audience, and they would get to see me play. It appeared I was the only one thinking that way. When the game moved into the fourth quarter, I got up and moved closer to the coach so he could see me. The game clock reached two minutes. My family started shouting my name; I thought for sure this was my chance to play. The clock reached thirty seconds, and I asked the coach to call time-out and put me in. My family was here, so I had to play. He kept eating his popcorn, and soon the game was over. This made me feel just as bad as the bus leaving me on the side of the road. In fact, it was similar to standing on the side of the road. I was alone again; giving up raced in my mind. I felt deeply that no one cared. It appeared that everyone in the gym was laughing since we won the game but me. As the players congratulated one another, the coach never said a word to me.

Now we were going home. The fans and team had enjoyed one another. Questions ran through my mind: *What will I say to my family? What will they say or do to tease me? What am I going to do—give up or keep pushing? Should I talk to the coach?* He was a nice man but seemed like he didn't care about me. This was the same type of feeling I had the day in Tucker when the sponsor didn't call my name to get on that bus traveling to Louisiana. I had to face my family like I had to face my mother and the community.

I went home and got into my bed and covered up my head. I didn't talk; I just hurt. There was nothing I could say to myself to ease the pains.

The next day I went to school and quit the team. I did this to avoid additional hurt, not realizing this was a setback to how I had first started highly motivated and full of confidence when I first went to this school. I went and told my cousin the principal that I was going to quit, hoping he would use his power to make the coach let me play the next time. In short, it didn't work. The reason I did this was because I heard my brother Asive say he told the principal; they had a meeting with the coach, and he ended up in the starting lineup. The difference was, Asive was a much better ballplayer than I was. At that point, I looked back over my life and determined it was a roller-coaster ride. Well, I got back on the team, but I still didn't play.

After a few days and weeks, I made a vow to myself: if I ever coach a team, I would find a way to make sure a child could say "I played." I guess I said this to make myself feel better.

What had happened was, my hurts drove me to think of ways to help prevent hurts in other children just like the vow I made that I would never let a child stand on the side of the road and not go on a trip if I could help it. As time passed during basketball season, I remembered my mother saying God knows how much you can bear.

Never give up. Wait on God. If you are going through hard times, read the poem "Footprints in the Sand":

> One night a man had a dream. He dreamed he was walking along the beach with the Lord. Across the sky flashed a scene from his life. For each scene he noticed two sets of footprints in the sand, one belonging to him and the other to the Lord. When the last scene of his life flashed before him, he looked back at the footprints in the sand. He noticed that many times the path of his life, there was only one set of footprints. He also noticed that it happened at the very lowest and saddest time in his life. This really bothered him, and he questioned the Lord about it. "Lord, you said that once I decided to follow you, you'd walk with me all the way. But I have noticed that during the most troublesome times in my life, there was only one set of footprints. I don't understand why when I needed you most, you would leave me."
>
> The Lord replied, "My son, my precious child, I love you, and I would never leave you. During your times of trial and suffering, when you see only one set of footprints, it was then I carried you."

This poem gives us the assurance that the Lord will never leave or forsake us. We can always trust him.

The Next Breakthrough
Because I Didn't Give Up

The school announced that there would be a talent-show night, so I formed a group. Their names were O.D. Kirkland Jr., Ruth and Georgia Brancomb, and myself. The group name was *Chunky and the —— (I don't remember the rest). But it was about me. I made this become that moment that I would be in the spotlight.

After weeks of practice, the talent-show night came. I'll never forget that night. We stepped out on the stage and sang "In the Still of the Night." I was the lead singer. The words of the song were soothing: "In the still of the night, I held you, held you tight, 'cause I love you, love you so. Promise I'll never let you go, in the still of the night."

I thought about the girl I lost to that young man years before. When I sang this verse, it created painful feelings. The words of the song were, "I remember the night in May the stars were bright above, I'll hope and I'll pray to keep your precious love will before the light. Hold me again, with all your might in the still of the night."

In this moment, as people were screaming, I felt alive. When I finished singing, my depressed feelings were lifted. On second thought, it looked like God knew what he was doing. He navigated a talent show for me.

When I left the stage, I felt, for once in my life, I was important. As I walked by, the audience, people were trying to touch me.

I said to myself, *I'm a star*. I enjoyed the moment.

Because I thought I was a star, I wouldn't let people touch me. Ain't that something?

This was long before I really learned what "life is filled with ups and downs" meant.

A month later, I found out without a doubt that life was up and down. I was brought back down. *New opportunities do not mean lasting success, but it can give you false thoughts.* The next day I was the same nobody. No one wanted to touch me or even speak to me.

A New Opportunity Came a Little Later That Year

The school was involved in an organization called the NFA (New Farmers of America). Every year there were various types of contests between schools. One of the contests was a quartet competition. I thought since I had thrilled the crowd at the talent show, becoming a quartet member was a sure in. There is a scripture in the book of Romans that warns us about thinking highly of ourselves: *"For I say, through the grace given to me, to everyone who is among you, not to think of himself or herself more highly than he or she ought to think, but to think soberly" (NKJV)*.

I tried out for the tenor spot. Boy, I was cocky. Nevertheless, I left crushed. It was not that I could not sing. My problem was that I could not keep my tenor note, so they cut me. I felt myself mentally standing on the side of the road. This time did not hurt as deep as the other times, but it hurt. It was as if I was becoming numb to pain. This can be dangerous. Something happened inside me. *This mindset told me not to surrender to the idea that I was on the side of the road. I reminded myself of a few things: "I am no loser. I am no quitter. I am a winner."*

This is a good mind game if you believe it. If I could convince myself, I would be okay.

After this fall, I knew I would get up more times than I fell. I learned from Sunday school Proverbs 24:16 (NKJV): "For a righteous man fall seven times and rise again." I didn't consider myself righteous, but I was influenced to rise again.

After I settled down a little, I decided to enter the talent number contest. I went to the teacher who would assign the talent number to a student. I volunteered to do the talent number at the NFA event. She asked me, "Didn't you try out for the quartet?" I thought this would rule me out. However, I responded, "Yes, ma'am, but I wasn't chosen." She did not say a word. She just looked. I assured her I could do the talent number. She kept looking me up and down. Finally, she said okay.

The song she gave me to sing was titled *"Be the Best of Whatever You Are."* How fitting was that song for a person who spent so much time of his life standing on the side of the road, who was doing all he could to fit in. I concluded that this song, "Be the Best of Whatever You Are," would make me become more focused on my personal abilities and talents. I could no longer focus on being who I was not.

The lyrics of the song are as follows:

If you can't be a pine on the top of the hill, be a scrub in the valley.
But be the best little scrub by the side of the hill.
Be a bush if you can't be a tree.
If you can't be a bush, be a bit of the grass, some highway happier make.
If you can't be a muskie, then just be a bass, but the timeliest bass in the lake.
If you can't be a highway, then be a trail.
If you can't be the sun, be a star.
It isn't by size that you win or you fail.
Be the best of whatever you are.

I didn't give up. I practiced and practiced. I didn't want to be hurt again. I was selected to do the talent number. I was the person who was laughed at, the person who was talked about and most of the time left feeling disappointed. I was always the one left standing on the side of the road. But now I was about to stand on a stage. Being selected was one victory. Just that one victory out of so many defeats made me feel good; I enjoyed that victory. Because after all my disappointments, my inner spirit, at this point, became like carbon steel. I branded myself as an overcomer.

I won third place in the talent number. I didn't pout about third place. I was just happy that I participated. So many people didn't place at all.

Years went by. I thought I had finally won the respect of others, but that was a dream. I lost girls whom I thought were sweet on me. One of the boys who took my girl laughed in my face. In fact, my hurts and pain never fully went away all the while I was in school.

It was now time for me to graduate from high school. I got my yearbook. I wanted to see what people really thought about me. Therefore, I was permitting people to write in my book. I was hoping to read inspirational words about myself, but to the contrary, I was voted most likely to fail. It was hurtful and disappointing. I thought I had impressed people. I thought I had arrived. Instead of crying, feeling despondent, I took this prophecy as a challenge to prove them wrong. I really didn't know what I was going to do, but I was not going to let anyone else define me.

The Challenges of How to Achieve Was the Big Question

How would I achieve greatness after just being average? I was an average student, average athlete, and average overall. I didn't stand out for my abilities. I spoke life into myself with these words: "If I'm going to prove people wrong, I will go to college and become a professional baseball player. I will make a lot of money. I will finally win respect and popularity." The following fall, I enrolled in college after my mother met with the president of the college to let her pay monthly on my siblings' and my tuition. I enrolled but was only able to take thirteen hours because I made low scores on all my entrance exams. But the good thing, I was in college.

After I got enrolled in college, my mind fell directly on baseball. This was my shot to become a somebody. I loved baseball, so I went out for the college baseball team. Then something struck me: What if I don't make the team? On the other hand, what if I do? With all of my doubts, I went out for the team anyway. To my surprise, I made the team, and my name was on the bulletin board. When I got my baseball uniform, I wanted to put it on and parade around in Tucker so everyone who ever laughed at me and remembered me standing on the side of the road could see that I was coming up in the world. They could not laugh anymore.

Dressed in my baseball uniform

Clark "Chunky" Thomas poses between innings.

John Dawson, Jerry Allen, Clark Thomas, Charles Cooper,
Jerry Smith—Outfielders and Infielders meet.

(1) Fellow teammates. I am standing in the middle.

The Roaring Lion Ball Club—FIRST ROW (L–R): James Buchanan, George Bolton, Dan Jones, William Cross, Billy Westbrooks, Fred Harris, Clark Thomas, Jerry Allen, Charles Cooper, Leroy Miller. SECOND ROW: Robert Jones, Jerry Smith, Willie F. Waugh, Charles Chancellor, Luthor Oliver, Verdell Roberts, Fred Lewis, Larry Richards, Fred Brown. THIRD ROW: Charles Harris (Manager), Allen Reed (Manager), James Cheathem, Leon Taylor (Co-Captain), Eddie Watson (Co-Captain), John Dawson, Elmer McKissie, Charles Loman, Coach Dedrick and Coach Spearman.

(2) Complete team. I am number 4, sitting from the right.

I went through the winter months of training, lifting weights, running, exercising, and throwing the ball trying to work on my skills. When spring came around, I learned I could be an occasional starter in opening season. I was one of the first to come out the bull-pen in relief. This meant that when the starting pitcher was taken out, I would replace him. I pitched against Southern University from Louisiana, Wiley College from Texas, Alcorn University from Mississippi, McMurray State, and a few others. I ended up earning a letter, which was a gold-and-black sweater. I learned one important lesson: *hard work pays off.* May I add, I didn't go out of state at thirteen, but God made it possible for me at eighteen years old to travel to several states.

When I look back over my life at that point, I got up more times than I fell.

The Next Year Was to Be My Year

The next year after my successful first year, I felt it would be my year to shine and make it big. I learned that professional baseball scouts had followed me during my first year.

I prepared for the upcoming year by practicing hard during the summer. When I entered school my sophomore year, things started to fall apart; things did not go well. I developed a groin injury. I became my worst enemy to my success; in fact, my success went to my head. I disregarded the importance of hard work. I made a habit of missing practice, which caused me to be more prone to injuries. Not only did I have a groin injury, I later hurt my rotator cup in my pitching arm. Instead of being able to throw a real hard fast ball, my pitches were slow and ineffective.

My testimony to anyone who wants to remain off the side of the road, dedicate yourself not to half-heartedly do things. Always put forth your best effort. Don't take shortcuts. Work hard.

My Dream Fell Apart

I tried to make it through the season and letter again, but something bad happened. I was starting pitcher against a team out of Illinois. I was leading in the game. A runner got on base because I walked him. When I faced the next batter, the umpire said I balked. To balk is the result of a pitcher making a certain move that the umpire deems illegal. That's when things started to fall apart. May I add, my father was in the stands. He had not ever seen me pitch, then this happened. My coach ran to the pitcher's mound. At first he was defending me, then immediately the coach started cussing me, took the ball out of my hand, and told me to get off his "D" field. As I walked from the pitcher's mound, he kept cussing me out. My father heard all this cussing. I went and sat down on the bench. He kept belittling me. Finally, my hurts and emotions overcame me, and I walked toward the coach with a bat. The coach was headed for his bag; they said he kept a gun in it.

Anyway, the team members and other coaches grabbed both of us. I had to give up my suit. My action was inexcusable, but all I could feel were pains like I had in my past years. I had become an embarrassment to myself and my father, and I soon realized I had destroyed my dream. *You cannot put spilled milk back into the bucket.* I left the field after the coach told me to go pull his uniform off. My father was wondering what had happened. The other team was laughing. I was back on the side of the road again.

Sometime later, the coach sent for me. He told me the umpire said he made a mistake. He told me I could get back on the team. I told him, after I had done a lot of thinking, if I got back on the team, it would be a distraction. I asked if I could return to the team next year. The next year was worse. I had cut classes and dropped classes.

37

When next season came, I did not have enough credit hours to play the upcoming season. My life was a mess. I had to face all the critics. What could I tell my mother? I had lost my scholarship. No more walking around with a uniform. This time no one else put me on the side of the road; I did it to myself. I was ashamed and afraid to tell my parents because I had let them down. My parents had invested in my education. My parents went to work sick, and now I was on the side of the road because I blew it.

When you are left standing on the side of the road because of anything you were involved in, the questions you need to answer are, Why am I in this position? Is it something I did, or did someone else cause it?

When I look back at my first major encounters, the time I was literally on the side of the road and watched the bus go by, it was not the sponsor's fault that I did not know four rivers in Arkansas. It was my own fault. Never blame others for your failures because when you do, success will always escape you. *Excuses are great cripplers to success.*

While Off the Team

While off the team, I totally convinced myself that it was all my fault and that I had always been responsible for having to stand on the side of the road. Especially not being able to be a part of the team. I looked back over my actions that helped me define my behavior after a heart-wrenching feeling that I had watching my fellow teammates and my brothers still playing and walking around in their baseball uniforms. At that point, I remade my commitment to strive harder to succeed. I decided I was going to use my pains to motivate myself and tell others that standing on the side of the road is a choice. I finally decided that as for me standing on the side of the road, it must be a thing of the past.

Even then, all I was going through placed me at a crossroads in life. Now the big question was, How do I actually stay off the side of the road? Since I was off the team, no scholarship, parents broke, and my grades low. I prayed to God for another chance to get it right.

As I faced another dilemma, my mother was there to help me.

My mother was there once again assuring me everything would be okay. *She had a saying that resonated with me: "Trouble don't last always, and the Lord will make a way."* When she said those things to me, once again she picked me up.

Advice to Parents

Parents, when your child is standing on the side of the road in pain, hurting, lost, and giving up, try a little bit of encouragement to help your child, which will give them something to hold on to. My mother gave me hope by showing me she cared. As time passed, time ushered in another disappointment. All I can say is, it happened again. My hope didn't last long. I had no money to go to school for that semester. I put my mother in an embarrassing position. She had to go to my uncle and ask him for money. He quickly turned my mother down. My mother came and told me when one door closes, God will always open another one.

Parents, Be Determined to Help Your Child

My mother had a seventh grade education, but she valued education. She was determined to help me and my siblings get back in school and keep me from what I would say ending back up on the side of the road. Even though she only had a seventh grade education, my mother somehow got an appointment with the president of the college. I felt this was a waste of time. My mother was not intimidated. She said she met with the president and told him the truth: "We don't have the money, and one of my children messed up. But if you let him go to school, we will pay you."

The president made a call to the dean of education and set up an appointment for my mother to visit with him. Again here was this country woman with a seventh grade education meeting with the dean of the college, a doctor of education. When my mother arrived at the dean's office, he already had completed my enrollment slip so I could start to school. Philippians 4:19 is a true scripture: "And my God shall supply all your needs according to his riches in glory by Jesus Christ." If you believe.

I asked my mother how she did it; she simply said, "Never doubt God." I still carry those words till this day. *Never doubt God!* My mother's efforts were fruitful.

I enrolled back in college with low grades as an ex-baseball player. I wondered, *How will I get off the side of this deeply abandoned road?* The answer was and still is NEVER DOUBT GOD. But I realized I must do my part. I must keep trying.

Back in School and How I Fared

During the fall semester, I was an honor student, and I carried enough hours to play baseball again. Would the coach want me back on the team? I whispered to myself, "Never doubt God." You got it! I made the team, and I even played and contributed to many wins. Never doubt God, even when you are on the side of the road. Never doubt God. When I got back on the team, I had an attitude adjustment. Psalms 119:67 (NKJV): "Before I was afflicted I went astray. But now I keep Your word, It is good for me that I was afflicted, that I may learn your status." This applied to me.

Standing on the side of the road created within me a posture of determination.

My standing on the side of the road always loomed big in my mind and what to do to help others who may end up on the side of the road. Therefore, the question was, What was I going to do about helping others off the side of the road? How would I prevent others from ever experiencing the "side of the road" hurts and pains? Returning to the team placed something in my spirit: *(1) God opened door to second chances; therefore, never waste a second chance.*

What I Did to Prevent Youth at the Age I Was from Being on the Side of the Road

I became the baseball coach of the Little League boys' team in my hometown of Tucker. Also I coached the women's softball team. There were individuals who did not have talent. I found a way to make them feel like they were valuable to the team so they could feel good about themselves

Later I started coaching third- to seventh-grade girls and boys basketball team. Many times, as I did in baseball and softball, I looked at the kids who had limited skills who wanted to play. I would find a way to let them be on the floor or being in the field and play for a few minutes.

Picture

(3) Picture of the older boys baseball team

(4) Picture of my Little League team

(5) Team members at the banquet; some of
the players' parents at the banquet

(6) Letters from former players

Coach Thomas

My experience as a Little League baseball player for Coach Ezell Clarke Thomas, better known as "Chunk"—a nickname given to him by his mother, Mrs. Laura. Coach Thomas. He was and still is a man I admire because of his obedience, respect, and humility. He is very hard-driven because he gives you 100 percent of himself. Coach was a class act by being a young man in college and playing baseball for AM&N. He took the time to share his love for the game with the young boys in his community, and thus BAGSBY DRUGS LITTLE LEAGUE BASEBALL TEAM was formed. He's not just a coach but adds structure to the lives of the team.

Now, as a player, I was a pretty good second baseman and made the allstar team two years in a row. Coach was one who hardly ever gave a boy praise because he wanted your best, and we tried to give it to him every time we played. So we were a pretty good team being from the country, but we were well coached. We often had to find a way to the game we were scheduled to play by any means necessary, and sometimes Mr. Enos Toney would fill in until Coach got there. But we got there, and we played and won. Coach taught more than baseball because he talked to us about God and also took some of us to church. That's where I met Mrs. Hazel from Tilla as we visited Pastor Cur-lee Thomas's church in Pine Bluff. Other than being a man of God, Coach Thomas also wrote plays and poems. He's a man who shows love and gratitude for God and his members by being the pastor of New Salem Baptist Church. So salute this servant of God and thank you, Coach, for being a part of my life as well as my brother's life by being a friend. May God bless you and keep you.

—Joe E. Roy (Second Baseman)

I played baseball for Pastor Clark Thomas (a.k.a. Chunk) for many years, from Little League to Pony League. If you could hit and couldn't or vice versa, you played. He was a developer.

I spent time with Pastor Chunk on and off the baseball field, learning how to rejoice in victory and learning from defeat. That's good coaching. Experiencing and giving respect begets being respected, and that builds character. He exemplifies the fact that the choices you make today will dictate your tomorrow. That good advice that makes a good leader for young people.

CLARK THOMAS

I have known Rev. Clark Thomas, a.k.a. Chunk, all of my childhood life. When he was a teenager, he was involved with the children in Tucker, Arkansas, in church and sport. Once, he tried to organize a community choir at St. Paul Baptist Church. He had a passion for sports and a desire to help the young boys and girls in Tucker to find their best fit. He was highly loved and respected by the parents in Tucker for what he was doing.

I played baseball for him and started out as an outfielder and also played second base. He had others who saw his compassion and assisted him as much as possible in coaching, and he allowed it, knowing they knew baseball as well as he did, like his brothers Joe and Alzavie, who showed me how to handle the bat being a left-handed batter. Milvin Clark was very instrumental in showing me how to hold my glove to catch the ball infield and outfield.

Clark Thomas was the mastermind with the vision to make the young boys and girls in Tucker be the best they could be. We were good in sports, especially baseball. He was good in football and basketball; he was just good in sports. Under his coaching, we were criticized by other teams because we were from Tucker, which is the home of the Tucker State Penitentiary, we were called prisoners. However, when we showed up in Pine Bluff at Townsend Park, the crowd showed up knowing it would be a great game.

He also wrote plays and got people in Tucker involved in acting. He was good at whatever he put his mind to. He inspired many young boys and girls in Tucker who are now grown men and women with children of their own, but the legacy of Clark "Chunk" Thomas lives on. He was my coach, my pastor, and my friend. I owe a lot to him.

—William Louis Tyler

(8) My baby boy

I wanted my son to grow up with confidence and a passion to excel. Therefore, he traveled with me to all activities.

(9) Third and fourth grade team playing at Humphrey
High School in Humphrey, Arkansas

These young people received great exposure to what it means to compete. They also learned how to accept victories and defeats gracefully. They never gave up.

(10) Third and fourth grade player doing time-out

(11) Some of my fifth- and sixth-grade girls player

(12) Letters from my former basketball players

Rev. Clark Thomas meant so much to me as a young child growing up. He was an awesome coach. He taught me the game of basketball and how to win and deal with losing. He did so much for me in my life. He is an awesome person, pastor, family man. Glad to have had a person of his caliber in my life. Thanks a lot, Rev.

—Reginald Tyler

My name is Tiffany Thomas, and this is my experience playing Pee Wee Basketball for my uncle Clark Thomas. First of all, I always got fussed at because he said I was lazy and didn't want to run laps and stay in condition. Overall, I enjoyed waking up on Saturday mornings riding in the van to go play tournaments at Wabbaseka-Tucker gym. I played point guard on the team. I felt like I was pretty good. We traveled to so many towns playing ball. My uncle was so good to all the players. If you didn't have money to eat, he made sure everyone ate at McDonald's. I'm so glad he pushed me also to never give up even if you're behind and not winning. Keep hustling until the last minute. Those were the good days of my childhood. I wish I could put him in the Hall of Fame of Pee Wee ball. I could go on and on about my coach, but it would take a lifetime of many beautiful stories. So let me end this by saying I wish I could go back in the day playing ball.

—Tiffany

If I knew then what I know now, I would have taken the teachings of my father and made my life decisions then easier. Since I didn't and took my lumps, it displayed his patience to allow me to learn and get to where I am now as a man.

This man gave his heart, soul, and life to me so I could have a foundation to build my current life on. That's why my father, Clark E. Thomas, is my hero. Forget about superman or other fictional character. My hero is real, and I can't thank him enough for the sacrifices he made while being in this position.

—Patrick Thomas

Rev. Clark Thomas introduced me to basketball. I remember playing Pee Wee Basketball under his leadership when I was just in the fourth grade. Back then, there was nothing like that for a young girl like me to do in my neighborhood, until he asked my mother if I could join his team. He went around the communities of Tucker, Gethsemane, Wabbaseka, and Ferda to form a girls and boys Pee Wee Basketball team.

He would practice with us on the weekends. I would be so excited to go and learn more about my favorite sport. He taught us the fundamentals of basketball at an early age. He taught us about the importance of conditioning to stay in shape so we would be able to compete. He also taught us about leadership, discipline, courage, and most of all, to respect and believe in ourselves.

He molded us into basketball stars and prepared us for the school varsity teams. He also taught us to be respectable young boys and girls.

I enjoyed every game, practice, and tournament that we had. It was a great experience, and I will remember it for the rest of my life.

Rev. Thomas was more than a coach; he was a great father figure for those who didn't have their fathers in their lives, such as me. He would often fuss at us when we were in the wrong or when we would mess up, but it was for our own good. His discipline made us better young girls and boys.

When we were in his care, he made sure that we all had food and/or money. He assured no child went without. I personally thank him for teaching me at a young age how to be a better basketball player and preparing me for the school teams.

I played from fourth to eleventh grades. I was a lover of the sport then, and I am still a huge basketball fan today.

Rev. Thomas was a great man of God, father, and teacher then and still is. I thank God for him!

—Tequila Flowers

(13) Letter from one of the women who
played on the women's softball team

Rev. Thomas, you may not remember this, but I will never forget.

When I started on my job and completed my training, I was assigned to Lonoke County for my first county. I had only been working about three years then. It was a *horrible* experience. My supervisor was very mean to me. I had never experienced such discrimination in my entire life. I drove home crying every day.

I thought about finding me a new job for a few days, and I finally decided to take off and go look for one and just quit FmHA. I worked up enough nerves to complete my leave request. I carried it into my supervisor's office for approval. By the time I left his office and before I got back to my cubicle, one of the clerks told me I had a phone call.

When I got back to my desk, I answered, "This is Vanessa. May I help you?" And you said, "Van?" I said yes. You said, "This is Chunk." I said, "Oh, hi, how are you?" And you said, "I am fine. I have been thinking about you for the past few days, and I am calling to tell you there are no jobs out there. I know things may seem tough on you right now, but it is not that bad. Hang in there, it will get better. Because it is tough out there. There are *no* jobs, and there are too many people looking. You got a good job with great opportunities, and you need to tough it out and keep it. You can do it. Things will get better. I will talk to you later." Then you hung up. I was *so* shocked. I had told no one my plans, yet you knew. I remember thinking, *God is really looking out for me.* So I tore up my leave request and continued to work.

I got to that point one more time, and as before, you called me with the same message at the same moment I decided to take leave to find another job. This time, I spoke to our district director and civic rights specialist. A few weeks later, I got transferred. That was over thirty-five years ago. I never thanked you for caring enough for me to take the time out of your busy schedule to talk me out of making such a terrible move. I always felt you were following God's instructions. Thank you for being obedient to his word.

I plan retire at the end of this year with thirty-nine years of service. I have over one year in sick leave, and if it be the Lord's will, it will make me have forty years of service. If you had not intervened those two critical times in my life and called me back to my senses, there is no telling where I would have been today.

I have never forgotten that. Nor have I thanked you for saving me. 😊

My love to you, and thank you too.

—Van

The Impact of My Past as a Player on My Coaching

I remembered how it felt. I would always recall the night I asked my coach to play just for thirty seconds, and he ignored me. These experiences are chiseled in my mind. These were episodic memories. I could never forget the pain. Therefore, I played kids to spare them the pains I felt. Everyone who reads this book, put care for others above the end results of yourself.

It is necessary to demand others to do their best. I also required each player to come to practice and practice hard. They knew they would play!

Each player on my teams had fun. The kids became a family. *No* one had to experience standing on the side of the road like I did because they played. A few years later, I stopped coaching, but some of my players who played basketball played on the high school championship teams. My standing on the side of the road motivated me to work with youths who never would have had a chance to play organized ball. Additionally, several of my baseball players had baseball scholarships.

My College and Baseball Days Were Over

I also used my motivation to start a female softball team along with a boys' basketball team. I also had a third to seventh grade girls' basketball teams.

Some Saturday when we had basketball tournaments, my wife, other parents, and I would have forty plus youth to supervise. All of this added value to my life.

The women's softball team was a winning group of women. These activities brought so much joy to each individual and the community. I applied the same principle about letting everyone play.

My baseball career was over. My dream to play professional baseball had ended. After I graduated college, "What now?" was the big question. Remember, I was the young man who finished high school voted "most likely to fail."

I now know never to let anyone define you. You must define yourself. I concluded I will not be someone who will be a failure. I knew I had to work hard because I wasn't the smartest person. I realized along the way that I needed to associate and connect with people who offer wise counseling and have the ability to sharpen me. As the scripture says, "Iron sharpens iron."

Even after I finished college, I still had low self-esteem. After college, I played semi-pro baseball and basketball. I excelled at both, but I needed pats on the back to help me to feel okay. I do remember two basketball games I played in. They were at St. Peter's school gym in Pine Bluff, Arkansas. One game that we played was against Cook's Chevrolet in the last quarter with six seconds to play. The ball was thrown into one player's hand, but it bounced off his hand

and landed into mine. I made a layup, and we won the game on the buzzer. Everyone was jumping up and down, which put me on cloud nine. I soon found out again that life is a moving picture; nothing remains the same. You can fall from cloud nine to rock bottom before you know it. This is what happened a few weeks later.

There was another tournament, and we were playing the same team but had different players. Once again the game was in the last quarter with a few seconds to play. Again the ball was in my hand. I dribbled toward the basketball goal as if I was going for a layup. The other team collapsed. I was going to pass the ball to my brother for him to shoot the jump shot, but before I could pass the ball, the other team's player grabbed me and threw me off balance. They took the ball from me, and the player went and made a layup on the buzzer and won the game. There was no jumping up and celebrating like it was the last game. In fact, I felt in my heart that my teammates were giving me the cold shoulder.

After that game, I felt lonely just like I felt the day I was left on the side of the road when I was thirteen years old. Even at twenty-two years old, I couldn't shake those inferior thoughts. I finally got over those painful thoughts that night of being a failure and how I knew I had let my team down. We played many more years of semi-pro basketball and were successful, but I never wanted the ball in my hand at the last seconds of the game. It's funny how negative things can impact a person's thinking. Nevertheless, this was a bright spot in my life. My time spent playing semi-pro baseball was fun. Many different teams sought me; this was a great feeling.

Three games in particular stands out. One Sunday we played a game in England, Arkansas. All three of my brothers and I were playing together. They were bragging about those Thomas boys. On this particular Sunday, we batted behind one another. James hit a home run to left centerfield, *Asive hit a home run to centerfield*, I hit a home run to left field, and Joe hit a triple to right field. At this time, my name was included with my other brothers about how good we were.

There was another game we played in England. I was playing second base. The back catcher tried to throw a runner out. The ball was low, so I tried to block it. It hit me in my privates and knocked me out, but not for long. The good thing about what happened was, I became the center of attention. My brother James was right there; my other brothers were not there that Sunday. I could hear everybody saying, "Is he all right?" I was loving it, so I put on a little show. I went to the hospital, and everything was fine.

I had one other high point in a ball game. It was at Stuttgart, Arkansas. My now wife of fifty plus years was there. I was pitching—I mean I was striking out batters after batters, and I could hear her saying, "Come on, Chunkie." That's my nickname. All these were fun times. Every piece of attention I received was welcome. In fact, I looked for it, and I needed it. I always needed affirmation.

What the Years Taught Me

One thing I learned through the years is, find something to do that will help you build your self-esteem. I became a basketball official. I figured out early how to gain what I was looking for; that made me feel successful. At officiations, I did not have the best basketball official mechanics, but I hustled to any position to make good calls. I got what I was looking for; they bragged on me. This was important to me. These games made me feel I had achieved something. The Good Lord put someone in my life that keeps my self-esteem up. I had the type of friend everyone with low self-esteem needs. Her name was Ella Mae Walker.

After every game, I called in her presence. She made sure I received words of affirmation that I was the best basketball official around. Just imagine how a person like me would feel who was always failing to measure up.

I had the mindset of Gideon from the Bible. "He felt he was a member a family that was least of the 12 tribes of Israel and he was the least in his family" (Judges 6:15). Gideon was encouraged by an angel of the Lord, who told him that he was a person of valor. That's what Ella Mae did for me by bragging on me as an official.

The sad news about Ella Mae is, she died at an early age.

After years of experiencing being on the side of the road, I learned many lessons.

The point I learned about being on the side of the road, failure in whatever you do, can create a "side of the road" feeling within you when you have low self-esteem. Also, I found out I must get engaged and not back away from a challenge. Only through successful victories over challenges can you build up your self-esteem. I always saw myself facing my inner fears as a person like King David facing the giant Goliath.

After I finished school, this David and Goliath situation happened in my life. I decided to run for a school board position against the most powerful white man in the district. At that time, there was only one black person on the board because the white people dominated the district. It was a tug-of-war in my mind. I thought, *If I lose the election, it will be like standing on the side of the road where people will be looking and judging me.* And my low self-esteem would take on a life of its own and probably grow into a monster. Being a person not sure of himself, this was a mind battle. Then I said to myself, *On the other hand, a victory would strengthen my self-esteem.* A strong, living, vibrant self-esteem is necessary for a person who once stood on the side of the road to be productive in life.

I Did Run for School Board

I decided to run for the school board, and not just to run but to *win*. During the race, something revealed itself, which was that genuine relationships can be counted on when the need arises.

It was those children whom I coached who became my volunteer workers. The children campaigned to their parents, older siblings, and other adults in the community. There wasn't anything they wouldn't do for me.

The many words I heard from so many people were, "Those kids really love you." I know this happened because I truly cared about them. When you experience standing on the side of the road, you know how to love, you know how to make people feel okay, and you know how to make people feel like they are somebody. As a reminder, these were the young people who played ball for me, those who had little or no talent, but they played. These were the young people who were treated equally, was never left out or forgotten about. They worked tirelessly for me. They didn't stand and pretend. They walked the roads daytime, evenings, and sometimes at night to help me win.

I will never forget the day of the election. It was raining, and my heart sank because people normally did not go to the polls in the rain. I developed a bad feeling that said I would lose the election and could end up a loser standing alone on the side of the road being talked about.

Amazingly, the early words of encouragement came to me from my kids, who said, "You're gonna win because our parents and siblings are voting for you." These young people became my encouragers. It is true that you reap what you sow. I sowed love, understanding, kindness—all that returned to me that day.

It was amazing to see how the people were coming and going. They were actually voting for me. With all the rain coming down, they still came and voted.

At the end of the day, after the polls closed, I had to wait to see how the votes were at the other poll places. A little later that night, the word came: I had won by forty-two votes. I said, "Wow, little nobody like me had won." I—the boy who nearly always stood on the side of the road—had beaten the most powerful man in the area.

A Special Helper That Day

A young very intelligent young lady by the name of JoAnn Alexander worked at the poll at my request. (Read the following information.)

Poll Watching: Not a New Phenomenon

A lot of attention was given to the role of poll watchers during the 2020 presidential elections. Poll watchers are citizens (ideally properly trained) who are charged with monitoring and observing polling places with the goal of rooting out irregularities or fraud in the voting process. Poll watching is not new.

Poll Watching in Small Town Arkansas

The setting is the Tucker Rosenwald school grounds, located in the small unincorporated town of Tucker, Arkansas.

One such poll worker was Joe Ann Alexander, an African American high school student. She recalls being seated in a vehicle outside Tucker Rosenwald School. It was an early fall morning sometime in the late 1960s, but prior to 1970. Voting was taking place at the school. Joe Ann's "job" was to observe and record happenings and circumstances associated with voting that was occurring at the school. She could not recall specific information she captured but does recall tracking the number of voters entering the polling place.

What Was Going On?
Why Poll Watchers?

The timeframe is the 1960s in the South. One obvious question is, What historical factors were occurring either locally within the state of Arkansas or in the "rest of the world" around this time? Specifically, what may have caused there to be the perceived need for "poll watchers" stationed at a voting locale in little ole Tucker, Arkansas?

One of the most historical events of that time was the passage of the Voting Rights Act of 1965, signed into law on August 6, 1965, by President Lyndon B. Johnson. The Voting Rights Act was aimed at overcoming legal barriers at the state and local levels that prevented African Americans from exercising their right to vote as guaranteed under the Fifteenth Amendment to the US Constitution. The Voting Rights Act is considered one of the most far-reaching pieces of civil rights legislation in US history.

On a local level and very personal and painful for many was the "voluntary integration/desegregation" of the two local public schools (Tucker Rosenwald and Plum Bayou). This leads to the question of whether the poll-watching efforts were somehow related to one of these. Was this about testing or monitoring the effectiveness of the Voting Rights Act, or was there a specific matter on the ballot impacting our community?

Regardless of the *why*, it is impressive that some members of our community were progressive-minded and brave enough to carry out this political action in the 1960s.

Who Spearheaded This Effort?

Who was the "radical," "activist," "rabble-rouser" behind this?

When Joe Ann Alexander was asked who recruited her to be a young poll watcher, she was able to say with certainty that this effort was spearheaded by Clark (Chunk) Thomas. Joe Ann went on to say, "I cannot recall specifically when or how my parents and I were asked if I would participate, but Rev. Thomas [known then to those in his community as Chunk] was our community activist. He was always and in my opinion continues to be ahead of his time, a fearless leader, and a generous spirit. He has been a lifetime role model for me, and this opportunity lit a fire in me to become a lifelong advocate for equal rights and equal opportunity. Thank you, Rev. Thomas."

Man, I won against Mr. C. A. of Plum Bayou.

(14) When I ran for our school board consolidated
with Wabbaseka, Arkansas.

While serving on the board after my first win, several things happened. Since the superintendent was white, along with the board members, they paid black teachers less than they paid the white teachers. In fact, the superintendent said, "The nigger teachers should not be paid as much as the white teachers."

I'm proud to say my determination and marching in protests brought about a change. Later that year, I received a death threat. After many years of serving in the district, the white community that once voted against me embraced me. This was a feeling I still cannot explain. I think I won them over because I always tried to be fair. I showed up at their houses. I worked for everyone. A street was named after me when the school district closed.

Things Changed After Many Accomplishments

Out of all the accomplishments and the districts consolidated, I was soon made to feel I was back on the side of the road. I was accused of manipulating favors for my wife. They said my wife went to college and was paid for work she did not do. I was also accused of spending money that was raised when we had Pee Wee Basketball games. My name, along with my wife's, was often in the newspaper. Many college administrative workers invaded my wife's college records.

At this time, I'm pastoring, but God always put someone in my life as an encourager. The member of my church walked beside me.

I went on to win several more terms on the board. The person, the most powerful man I won against, became my friend.

During the period of being a board member, I fought for these kids who could not fight for themselves. I also fought for teachers, janitors, coaches, bus drivers, etc. These people to me were on the side of the road because they really did not have a voice. I knew how they must have felt. After being talked down to as black people, they made less money than their white counterparts did.

New Salem church members where I pastor.

Anytime you are on the side of the road, you need an encourager to lift you up. My members said many times, "We do not believe this, and we are praying for you." My pastor said something to me that helped. He said God always takes the meaning out of a lie.

After a few months of going backward and forward, my name and my wife's name were finally cleared. That scripture is true: "No weapon formed against you will prosper."

Recommended Outlet for Anyone Who Finds Themselves Standing on the Side of the Road

As I lived through my teen and adulthood years, I discovered an outlet for my hurtful emotions. Feeling lonely, I began to write plays. I put my feelings on paper. I would write about the actions a person needed to take to be an overcomer in the play. In fact, the plays were about my life or real events I witness. The first play I wrote was titled *The Inexperienced Boy*. I had fallen in love with a young lady, and I tried for months to show her my feelings by being respectful to her, but I did not connect because my conversations were not challenging. When I think about it, they were elementary. I showed a lack of confidence. I dressed like a nerd. To top it off, I was not handsome like the guy she fell in love with. Therefore, I put the way I felt in playwriting. It enabled me to write down the steps on how I wanted the outcome to be. I wrote down that it was okay to be yourself even if you were not accepted by your age-group. I wrote in the play how my consistency of being popular helped me earn respect from the girl I really wanted. I knew this was not real life (it was a play). I was able to see it was the type of ending I wanted to happen.

After writing the play, I received so many compliments. This was great for my self-esteem. Because of the success of the play *The Inexperienced Boy*, I wrote another play titled *In the Ghetto*. I wrote this play about the pains I had seen. They were racism pains my community was facing after being forced to attend an all-white school. I used that play as a motivator to build my courage to stand for those young people who were always there for me and the parents who stood in the rain to vote for me.

That play featured a young man who saw a need in his community, but no one was stepping up. He became an activist, organizing against white mobs. In the play, he was later killed, but his legacy lived on. It was and still is my dream to help people get off the side of the road. At that time, Dr. MLK was my idle.

The auditorium was full, and the play was a success. I received numerous accolades. However, I did overhear someone say my play was racist. A few days later, my mother was called and told I had been killed. There was some fear in me, but it was not as bad as when I was left standing on the side of the road. This play created a sense of self-worth in me.

I still write plays at the church I pastor. Some of the plays I wrote include *When Is a Man a Man*, *The Loving Father*, *The Danger of Putting Off*, and many, many more. Each play was designed to help me deal with some pain that could possibly cause me to be on the side of the road.

I Kept My Promise

I said early in the book that after standing on the side of the road with deep hurt, pain, and shame, I made a promise. I promised the Good Lord that if he put me in a position to help prevent anyone from standing on the side of the road, hurting like I did, I would do whatever it took to help any child who wanted to travel somewhere in the US so they could broaden their knowledge. I also promised that night that I would do all I could to help anyone. Then I made a deeper vow: I would help anyone with my finances who may feel left out just because they did not measure up or have the resources.

The opportunity came for me to keep my promise. God had placed me as pastor at New Salem Church at the age thirty-two. Little could I believe my dream about traveling and carrying others on trips would soon come true.

I proposed to the leadership after a year or two of being their pastor that I wanted to institute a traveling ministry where young people could go places, be exposed to new things, and create a true fellowship with one another. The Lord opened that door. We did not have a van or bus, but we had a group of people the Lord had his hand on.

The first trip was to a little park by the Arkansas River. The town was called Tamo.

How were we able to go? That was the big question. The answer: the members used their cars and vans. After it was over, the Lord caused such excitement about the trip everyone wanted to do it again. I said to myself, This had to be the way the children felt when they were on the Trailways bus headed to Louisiana.

The next year, we had a church picnic in Little Rock, Arkansas. Again the Lord laid his hand upon the members. They used their cars and vans. It was another successful trip. The first trip's distance was about thirty-three miles from the church. The second trip's distance to Little Rock was about fifty miles from the church. I had only gone there once when I about twelve.

The beauty of the second trip was, many of our children and some adults had not been to Little Rock. The pains from standing on the side of the road and the vow I made to make sure others travel seemed to be paying off.

My next idea, I thought, would cause a death to the traveling ministry. I proposed going to Hot Springs, Arkansas, where the Magic Springs amusement park was located. I told them it would cost a little money. I proposed the trip a year in advance, and I told them how much it would cost. Again the Lord laid his hands upon our members. Everyone paid a little when they got the chance; then I asked the church to donate $500 toward the trip. When the time came, we had enough money, and the members once again used their vehicles. When we arrived in Hot Springs, people were ecstatic. I felt like a little child at Christmas. I hadn't ever been to that park.

After the Hot Springs trip, I decided I must try and cause something to happen for the children that I did not experience at their young age. I wanted to carry them out of state. I went back to our leader and asked if we could go to Memphis, Tennessee. I said, "Let's carry our children out of state." They wanted to know where we were going to. I told them Liberty Land. They agreed, but then they asked how we were going to get there and how much it would cost. This created a big concern for me because I knew I didn't have the money to make it happen. I became afraid; there was one deacon who scared me to death. I prayed.

A while later, I gave them the price, and I said this would include riding on a bus. I proposed doing a cookout and asking for sponsors. The Lord made it happen for us again. I remembered what my mother said: *never doubt God.*

I knew the Lord was in this ministry because so many other churches tried this but didn't succeed. I must also say the members of the church as a whole were forward-thinking people; but on the other hand, I didn't know if I was pushing God too far. Again the saying of my mother kept coming to me: *never doubt God.*

Since I thought God was in it, I decided we should take a longer trip and spend the night. I braced myself for resistance. This time I proposed St. Louis, Missouri. After much prayer and after speaking to the people, I heard back from them. Some of the people were concerned about the children's behavior, but I said, "Let's see what will happen." Then they said, "This will cost too much." After praying continually like Nehemiah, I suggested that we do more cookouts and again get sponsorships. I encouraged members to pay a little every month, and it happened. We chartered a bus, Arrow Coach Line, and we actually stayed in a hotel. We went to Six Flags. The children were very respectful. This was the first time many of the members had been to St. Louis, Missouri. I truly started to believe that my standing on the side of the road was a blessing in disguise.

After these trips, we saw relationships being built. The children's conduct was not perfect but were commendable. The scripture where Jesus said, "Suffer little children to come unto me," I took this statement to mean give children a chance.

Comment from a Traveler

I was afforded the opportunity to travel on many church trips starting at a young age, even until I became an adult. We traveled across the US. The list of all the destinations is long. I was raised in a large family, living in a home with my grandmother and cousins. Our home was full of love, but money was not the case. In my opinion, Rev. Clark Thomas created these trips because he knew that some of us would never be able to afford or experience life outside of where we grew up. I learned on these trips how to conduct myself away from home. Money-management skills is also something I learned. The little money I had to take on the trip with me, I had to make that stretch for the entire trip.

Fellowship is another important aspect I gained from these wonderful trips. This world is too broad to think life and situations only exist according to this small box created with you and your family. Traveling on a bus, staying in a hotel, visiting many attractions, dining at restaurants, all these things taught me how to interact with people that I am not normally with daily. In conclusion, those trips will always be special to me because they taught me life lessons. Thank you, Rev. Clark Ezell Thomas for including me. You really have no idea.

—Tonya Gray

When thinking about one exact memory or experience I've had on the church trips I've been on, I realize it's quite difficult to narrow it all down. There is, however, one thing that I will remember forever, and that's how much those trips meant to me. Growing up, I've seen and gone through a lot of things that I always dealt with internally. My school and personal life didn't help much because my daily routine throughout my life was the same, which now that I look at it makes me feel like I was just living in the environment of my problems on a daily basis. When I was gone on church trips, things were different. I didn't have many problems because I was in shock of how beautiful the cities were. I never thought I'd visit places like these. My family was happy, I was happy, life was great. From the morning prayers to the bus malfunction, I enjoyed every moment. Hopefully the world will get back to being normal so I can take my little brother one day.

—Jerron Gray

Comments about Play

My name is Lorice Eason-Wiggins. I really enjoyed participating in those Christmas plays. I enjoyed everybody, and we had a lot of laughter together. I just loved those Christmas plays. They meant a lot to me. I will never forget them.

—Lorice Eason-Wiggins

My name is Rev. Kenya Wiggins. I enjoyed playing in every play. Every one of the plays was exciting and meaningful. I learned from each play. I had lots of fun. My wife and I were partners in all the plays we were in. I enjoyed working with her at home and at the church, and I also enjoyed working with other church members who participated in the play. We were just like one big family.

—Rev. Kenya Wiggins

Church Trip

My name is Lorice Eason-Wiggins. The church trips meant a lot to me. The places I'd never been to before and people I'd never seen were a blessing. I enjoyed it, getting to know my church members and building a relationship with one another. I thank God for putting people to be part of my life. Thank you.

—Lorice Eason-Wiggins

My name is Rev. Kenya Wiggins. The church trips meant the world to me. I was able to go to cities and states I'd never been to.

—Rev. Kenya Wiggins

Additional Benefits
from the Trips

Not only were relationships built, but the exposure introduced our children to new knowledge. In fact, several of the kids said, "I want a house that big." Come to find out it was a hotel. At this point, I knew that exposure builds knowledge.

When I saw all this happening, I knew it was worth the effort and the cost. That standing on the side of the road was a Godsent event in my life. I just could not see it at that time.

The next two years was a dream for me. We decided to take trips to Atlanta, Georgia, and Pensacola, Florida. The cost for these two trips were great. This time, my wife and I started paying children's way who came from families who simply didn't have the extra money. We had many in the church who would donate money. We also had an elderly deacon, Brother Elwin (Jack) Smith, who went on trips with us who supervised children during summer who worked the cedar program, which was a government summer program that afforded work for youth at a certain age, which helped them earn money to pay their way.

Another Standout Lady in the Area Assisted Greatly

There was a lady who lived in the community by the name of Mrs. Jimmie Lee Edwards. She was a true philanthropist with her emphasis on children. She owned land where she raised many vegetables. She would permit children to work for her, and she would give them extra money for their effort so they could pay their way on the trips. She would also donate money on the side. When I stood on the side of the road, I could never picture people being kind. As I went through my other hurts and pain, I branded people as being hateful.

More Details About Trips

I have to say I acted like a little child on many of these trips. It was the first time I had been to a number of these states. These are pictures of some of the trips we went on.

(15) First trip to a little place called Tamo, Arkansas

Travelers to the trip to Six Flags over Texas

(18) Creations Museum in Kentucky

(19) Chattanooga, Tennessee

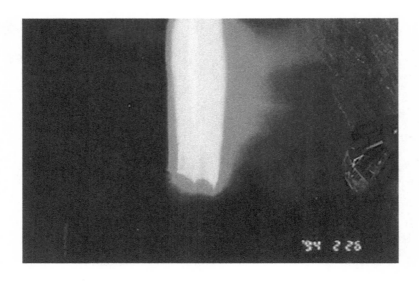

Ruby Ridge at Chattanooga, Tennessee, in the underground level

Underground cave in Chattanooga, Tennessee

Traveling to the Aquarium in Chattanooga, Tennessee

(21) Additional pictures of the Aquarium in Chattanooga, Tennessee, and our group traveling to the site

Standing outside of Madison Square Garden where my youth sing.

Pictures of children singing on the steps at Madison Square Garden

Young ladies who traveled on the trip are standing
outside the hotel in New Jersey.

(22) Myself standing with our church musician
and young ladies in New Jersey

Myself and wife when we traveled to New York
and visited *Good Morning America*

Virginia Beach

At Virginia Beach

At the amusement park in Atlanta, Georgia.

(20) At the amusement park in Atlanta, Georgia

At the Martin Luther King Museum in Atlanta, Georgia

When we visited the Martin L. King Museum in Atlanta, Georgia

We went to a graduation of one of our youths that took
place at Morehouse College in Atlanta, Georgia.

Harpo Studios, *The Oprah Winfrey Show* in Chicago, Illinois

London Fog, Canada

Baptizing that took place in Mobile, Alabama,
in the hotel's swimming pool

Baptizing that took place in San Antonio,
Texas, in the hotel's swimming pool

The US Capitol, a place we visited several times

(23) Trip to Florida. I am standing beside my daughter, who later passed away from COVID.

This is a picture of my daughter and me. We were standing
outside the Broadway Theater in New York.

There were many other trips we made that cost plenty, and when some of our elderly members got a little upset because they thought I was working hard for them but was leaving them out. Then I told the church my story about standing on the side of the road. Passionately, I told them about the promise I made to God. This, at least, stopped the vocal attacks. Afterward, I shot big. I wanted to go places and stay out five to six days, and it happened. *Never doubt God.*

We visited places that I personally never thought I would ever go to. Just to list a few, God opened doors for us to travel to Washington, DC, New York, Minnesota, Kansas City, Colorado, Oklahoma, Texas, Alabama, North Carolina, South Carolina, Kentucky, Ohio, Michigan, Canada, Virgina, Pennsylvania, Maryland, Virginia, and New Jersey. To the many of the places mentioned, we went more than once. At no time did we leave anyone standing on the side of the road.

Great Things Happen on the Trips

Some great things happen on the trips: Young people accepted Christ on the bus. We baptized in hotels swimming pools. We visited many educational sites: Fort McHenry, Dr. King's Museum, nation's Capitol, the Apollo, and Madison Square Garden. In fact, our children sang on the steps of the Madison Square Garden and on the stage of the Apollo. We fed people who were homeless, gave money to needy families.

There were several scary things that happened during some of our trips. It was in Washington, DC. My son and nephew got lost in a red-light area, which is a bad area. I asked the police for help. He asked me what area my son was in, and I told them. His response was, "I hope you find him alive." Some of the boys on the trip went with me looking down alleys and dark areas, and we finally found them. They said, "We never left the lighted area after we saw a lady being beating up by a man." The second thing that happened: I took seriously ill in Alabama, which was miles away from home and my doctor. *The children were crying. People were openly praying. My wife and my children were scared.* There was a nurse on the bus who was a member of the church who had my doctor's phone number. She made contact with him, and he called in medicine at a Walmart in Mississippi. After getting and taking the medicine, I finally got okay. Lastly, our members went to Amateur Night at the Apollo. It was great. This was a result of me standing on the side of the road and God using my experiences to make a difference in other people's lives.

My "standing on the side of the road" experience would not let me quit traveling. I always believe there's a boy or girl wanting to board a bus and go.

After years of traveling with the youth, jealousy broke out in the church from the elderly. The senior citizen who had complained early on started to complain again and said that all I cared about was the youth. The Lord stepped in and helped me begin a senior-citizen traveling ministry. The seniors didn't know that was also a promise I made to God, which was to help seniors go places. The reason for this thought was, my mother and father were too poor to travel. I talked to the leaders of the church and told them what I would like to do. I proposed to carry our seniors on trips at no charge to them. I proposed carrying them around to places in Arkansas and paying for their food. We went to many great sites. Some of our trips included going to the Golden Corral to eat, Texarkana, Arkansas, Fort Smith, Fayetteville, Bentonville, Hot Springs, DeGray Lodge, President Clinton Library, and much more. I have included some pictures.

(24) Pictures of the senior citizen trip. One picture is to Hot Springs, Arkansas; and the other is in Memphis, Tennessee, on Bill's Street.

Picture 4a

(27) Another group of senior citizens that was taken on Bill's Street in Memphis, Tennessee

(26) Two sisters who traveled with the senior citizens

This picture was taken in Louisiana.

Details About the Senior-Citizen Trips

We started the traveling ministry for our seniors at no cost. I would contribute portions of my salary that the church gave me every week to help with the cost. A few members would donate a little. These donations helped us start traveling out of state.

On our trips, even when we traveled in Arkansas, I saw members who had problems with one another start to talk and sit together on the same seat. The seniors went many places out of state such as Oklahoma; St. Louis, Missouri; Nashville and Memphis, Tennessee; Texas; New Orleans; and Branson, Missouri several times to see stage plays. As they got older, we would just go out to dinner and breakfast. I had several of my seniors who felt church was a strict place and later said they wish they had known long ago that you could also have fun being a Christian.

Because of my "side of the road" experience, it helped me become a servant of people and truly recognize the power the Lord.

I challenge anyone who feels they are standing on the side of the road to practice Proverbs 3:5–6, which says, "Trust in the Lord and become a cheerful giver." My advice as parents, children, leaders: always use your negatives as a motivator to do greater things. Avoid becoming bitter. Nothing good happens when a person acts in bitterness. When things go wrong, don't become paralyzed in self-pity. Always remember you cannot recover spilled milk from the ground and put it back into the bucket.

When life seems to be getting the best of you, buckle down and fight those negative feelings. Surrendering should never be an option. Every step I made to do better was a fight.

I hope this book will serve as an encouragement to anyone who feels they were or are standing on the side of the road in life not to give up but push and fight until God opens your doors of opportunities to do great things. Another point I want to repeat: never look for excuses to blame others when you find yourself standing on the side of the road.

I challenge every reader who may be standing on the side of the road or may one day find themselves on the side of the road to commit striving for better. Your ultimate goal is to thrive. As for me, I know my thriving came because of God and surrounding myself with loving, caring family members and friends. Additionally, all I achieve included *always* helping others to enjoy and appreciate life.

Questions to answer to determine if you may be standing on the side of the road:

1. Do you feel like an oddball in your family and among friends?
2. Are you overlooked when events take place?
3. Do you feel inadequate when you look at yourself in the mirror?
4. Do you wish many times in life that you were someone else?
5. Do you feel angry a lot?
6. Do you wish you could start life all over again?
7. Are you in the habit of blaming other people for what you don't have?
8. Are there things in your life that created some hurts and pains you can't forget?
9. Have you given up on succeeding in life?

If your answer to many of these questions is yes, then you are a candidate to find yourself as a person standing on the side of the road. Hopefully this book will provide a blueprint of what to do to move forward from standing on the side of the road to becoming someone with purpose and destiny.

PINE BLUFF

91ST YEAR NO. 71 (AP) — Associated Press PINE BLUFF, AR
Los Angeles Times-Washington Post News Service

Recreation Program Gets Under Way at Tucker

Horseshoe pitchers vie for a trophy. Some 2000 persons turned out at the old Tucker Rosenwald School yesterday to kick off a recreation program sponsored by the Tucker Community Recreation Association. Softball and volleyball teams from Stuttgart, Pastoria and England competed for five trophies. Clark Thomas, president of the association, and Mrs. Lucreasia A. Evans, secretary-treasurer, said the facilities were provided by the association with the help of Arkansas Power and Light Company, Wilson Funeral Home of England, the Tucker Water Association and the Office of Economic Opportunity. The group plans to have some sort of activity each Saturday during the summer and to increase playground facilities at the school, being remodeled as a community center.

Picture of young people having fun at a recreation center I was able to get started and later named after my mother by the Jefferson County judge.

Appendix 1

This is part of my story I did not put in the body of my book because I wanted this to be my greatest advice to the readers who do not have a relationship with Jesus. At the age of fifteen, in the midst of a struggling time in my life, I gave my life to Jesus. My mother told me many times during my struggles to just pray to God, and he would fix it, but first you need to be saved and baptized. This made little sense to me. I asked her how was I to do that, being saved? She said, "Find yourself a private praying place and ask God to forgive you of your sins and save you." None of it made sense to me, but I tried it.

During this time, there was a revival in the community. My mother said, "Now you can get on the mourners' bench." I thought to myself, *What in the hell is that?* I later found out this was the place where people who wanted to be saved and not go to hell sit in front all of the people. When someone came to pray for you, everyone would get on their knees, and they would pray for God to touch you and make you feel something. You had to be careful while on your knees; you could fall asleep. When they finished praying, we would get up, and then the preacher would preach about hell, and he would really scare the hell out of you. Once he finished preaching, they would ask you if you believe in Jesus and exchange seats. I had prayed all that week after I had been told to select someone in the church I had faith in to pray for me. I did. That Thursday night, something really happened to me on the inside, and I exchanged seats. I was later baptized.

Why did I share this short story? It was at this point in my life when I was ashamed to talk to anyone about my struggles. I took my mother's advice and talked to Jesus. I admit it still didn't make a lot of sense to me, but after I talked to Jesus, I really felt better. Now I know even in my ignorance Jesus really heard me and was working behind the scenes in my behalf.

I highly recommend that anyone struggling with low self-esteem, about to give up on life, to consider giving their life to Jesus and develop a consistent prayer life. Those people who may have given their life to Jesus but feel that it was a waste of time, they should embrace the words that my mother told me: NEVER GIVE UP ON GOD, and they should study the promise of God.

Try Jesus.

Sample Play
Putting Off

MOTHER, *walking while holding the baby James*. When little James gets older, I want to be able to say we have the perfect child.

JAMES I, *smiling*. I know, and if I have anything to do with it, he will not be like old George's two boys (*pause*). Since we are going to Alaska for a few years, he'll really be polished.

James goes to get suitcases. They leave.

NARRATOR. James Sr. and his family have been in Alaska for five years. I wonder how little James Jr. is doing.

Mother and father enter carrying suitcases. Junior enters playing with a yo-yo.

JAMES SR. Junior, go bring in your bags.

JUNIOR. Okay! (*continues to play*).

MOTHER, *coming out*. Junior, have you gotten your bags?

JUNIOR. No, ma'am, Mama. I'll get them.

Mother leaves.

JAMES SR., *enters*. Didn't I tell you to go get your bags (*goes to door*). It's raining now!

JUNIOR, *walks in Daddy's face*. I'm sorry!

JAMES SR., *looks at Junior*. Come on, let's go to the other room and play on your machine.

NARRATOR. As time went by, James Sr. and his wife continued to work with Junior. They were trying to make him the perfect child. Several years have now passed. Junior is still putting things off.

One evening after school, Mother fixes Junior a snack and a place to study.

JAMES SR., *enters.* Judy, how is Junior doing in school?
MOTHER. I'm going to see his teachers Monday.
JUNIOR, *enters.* Hi, Mom. Hi, Dad!
MOTHER: Do you have any homework?
JUNIOR. Yes, ma'am, Mother. I have to turn it in by tomorrow.
JAMES SR. That's my boy. Judy, I told Junior we are leaving for a while. You can have the house and work on your lessons.
JUNIOR. Sure, Dad. (*Mom and Dad leave. Junior gets books out, eats, then looks at his watch.*) It's early, I got time. Let me call Larry (*goes to phone and dials*). Hello, Larry? You getting your homework out? Am I? No... I'll do it later... Did you see that good-looking new student?... You must go? (*Hangs up the phone and starts to listening to music. He falls asleep, books in hand.*)
JAMES SR., *enters.* Look at my Einstein!
MOTHER. Junior, wake up and go to bed.
JUNIOR. What time is it? Let me finish my lesson.
MOTHER, *about to leave.* The teacher has given you a big assignment. Make sure you get it.
JUNIOR, *bows his head and reads awhile.* It's twelve o'clock. I'll get some sleep and get up early and do my lesson.

The next morning:

JUNIOR. Oh my (*running out*), I got up late. The bus is about to run. I'll let this teacher know how sorry I am. Maybe he'll forgive me.

NARRATOR. It's now Saturday morning. Mother and Father are gone.

JUNIOR, *talking on the phone* (*he has a two-way*). Just a minute, Larry, someone is calling. Hi, Mom, check and see if the iron was left on. Okay! (*Click back to Larry*). That was Mom... Say, man, are you going to the Greek show next week? You going to church? Hold on...(*pretends like he smells something, jumps up and runs, comes out with a dress burned, then goes back to phone*). Man, Mama left the iron on and burned her dress.

Father and Mother enter.

MOTHER. Junior, what's burning? Did you turn the iron off when I told you?
JUNIOR. Mama, I'm sorry.

Junior leaves. Mother and Father stay in.

MOTHER. Have you noticed for the past fourteen years Junior just puts off and puts off doing things? And when he gets caught, he feels saying "I'm sorry" will fix it?
JAMES SR. Why don't we call him in here and tell him? Junior! Junior! Come out here!
JUNIOR. Yes, Dad?
JAMES SR. Your mother wants to talk to you about something.
MOTHER. James (*looking at her husband*) Junior, I've noticed how you put off doing things and then say "I am sorry" when called into question. Junior. one day this putting off is going to get you into much trouble.
JUNIOR. Mom, I've NOTICED that about myself, and I'm going to change.
JAMES SR. That's my boy. I told you he'll be better than any of these boys around here.

NARRATOR. They all leave.

Four years later...

MOTHER. Junior, I've just left the school, and the teacher said the report that was due last week was not turned in. In fact, they said you are always late with your lesson.

JUNIOR. Mom, I'm sorry.

MOTHER. Sorry (*pauses*), well, I fixed it. They said if you turn in the lesson by tomorrow, you will be able to graduate.

JUNIOR. Mom, I'll do my lesson tonight. I—

MOTHER. NOW!

JAMES SR. Is my graduate the val or sal?

Mother and Junior look at each other.

MOTHER. Let's hope he graduates.

JAMES. He will (*leaves*).

MOTHER. Let's go to your room, *Junior* (*they leave*).

NARRATOR. Well, Junior graduated. Now at the age of twenty-eight, he moved out. He has landed an accounting job. Hopefully he is doing well. Junior and his boss are coming to the house.

BOSS. Say, Junior, I need these ledgers balanced by six o'clock today.

JUNIOR. Sure, boss.

BOSS. Remember, I'll be back at six o'clock. I have a meeting with the chairman of the cooperation.

JUNIOR. I promise (*raises his right hand and starts spreading his papers out; looks at his work then at his watch*). I've got four hours. I need to relax first (*he falls asleep* and *later wakes up*). It's five thirty (*really working hard*).

Boss knocks on the door. Junior doesn't answer and continues to work.

BOSS, *hollows out*. Say, Junior, this is Joe Hart, your boss.

JUNIOR, *standing up*. Here I come (*working*), just a minute (*goes to open the door*).

BOSS. Is the ledger ready?

JUNIOR. No, I haven't finished.

Boss. I'm meeting with the chairman in twenty minutes.
Junior. I'm sorry.
Boss, *grabs the paper*. I am too. You're fired!

Narrator. A few years later, after Junior had had a wreck, he got a good settlement from the insurance company.

Junior, *on the telephone*. Joyce, I can't come by tonight. I promised Sally I would carry her to the Greek show. Tomorrow night? (*looking at a schedule book*)... No, I'm going over to Mary's house for cocktails. I'll call you back (*laughing*).

There is a knock at the door.

Junior. Come in!
Preacher, *enters*. Hello, Mr. Bray.
Junior. My, Preacher, you had a powerful message Sunday! And, Preacher, I love the way you tune in and throw that coat!
Preacher. That's not what I wanted you to remember about the sermon. Have you ever thought about where you are going to spend eternity?
Junior. You know, Pastor, I was just thinking about that. What choices do I have?
Preacher. Heaven or hell.
junior. Pastor, I want to go to heaven.
Preacher. Then you need to do what I said in my sermon: believe in the Lord Jesus Christ and all the work he did for all of us.
Junior. You're talking about him dying on the cross and getting up out of the grave?
Preacher. Yes! If you can believe that Jesus Christ is the Son of God, you can be assured that you'll spend eternity with God.
Junior. Oh, I've always believed that.
Preacher. Are you willing to openly confess him tonight at our prayer service?
Junior. Rev, I think I will... I'll be right over.
Preacher. I'll see you there.

JUNIOR, *goes to get his coat and thinks.* I can't go tonight. I've got to go to the Greek show (*starts combing his hair and putting on cologne, then he goes to phone*). Say, Sally, come by in a couple of hours and pick me up. I want to rest a little while.

Junior sleeps all night. The preacher knocks on door.

JUNIOR. Come in.
PREACHER. Mr. Bray, we waited on you. What happened?
JUNIOR. Pastor, I promise you I'll do it Sunday.
PREACHER. I'll be waiting.
JUNIOR. I promise. In the meantime Brother Pastor, I'm getting ready for a date. I'll see you.

The pastor leaves, and Sally shows up.

SALLY, *knocks on door and enters after being ushered in.* Junior, let us go so we can get a good seat where we can see.
Junior looks confused.

SALLY. What is wrong with you?
JUNIOR. The pastor came by talking about Jesus and going to heaven or hell. Have you done that stuff…you know, saying stuff at the church about Jesus?
SALLY. I surely did. If I die, I know I'm going to heaven. I did not put that off.
JUNIOR. I think I'll do it Sunday. I didn't feel like it last night.
SALLY. Maybe you need to go talk to the pastor now before we go out.
JUNIOR. I will see the pastor tomorrow. That's only a few hours away.

They start to leave, but a stranger shows up.

PERSON. Do you know life is short and unpredictable?
JUNIOR. Who are you?
PERSON. Just say I'm a person who was sent to tell you not to put off accepting Jesus as your Savior.

JUNIOR. I don't know who you are. I do not care who you are. So get out. We have somewhere to go.

PERSON. Do you know, after while is not promised to you or anyone else?

JUNIOR. Look at me. Look at this body. I got time. I am not sick. I do not even take medicine.

PERSON. If you say so. You do know that after death there are no second chances.

JUNIOR. Who are you?

PERSON. I was sent by someone who loves you to encourage you to accept Jesus as your Savior.

JUNIOR. My mama and daddy are dead. I don't know anyone else. Who really cares?

PERSON. The person who sent me loves you even in your mess—

JUNIOR. Just leave (*opens the door and points to it, leaves*).

PERSON. Just don't put off (*looking back*).

SALLY. Are you an angel?

The person leaves.

JUNIOR, *laughs*. An angel looking like that. Let's go!

SALLY. Angels of God always bring divine news. Do you have an asthma pump?

JUNIOR, *hits his pocket*. I forgot I didn't take time to pick it up at the drugstore.

SALLY. Junior, you put off too much. One day your putting off will catch up with you.

JUNIOR. I don't need your lecture, Sally. I think that drugstore is still open. On second thought…girl, I will get it tomorrow. (*They leave.*)

PERSON, *reenters*. You do not know the day nor the hour when the Son of man will come.

The song "I Don't Know About Tomorrow" plays. Minutes later…

SALLY, *screaming*. Help, somebody, help!

The person leaves.

SALLY. He cannot breathe (*helps Junior back into the house*).

The person reenters with an asthma pump and gives it to Sally.

SALLY. Who are you?
PERSON. Just help him.

Sally helps Junior to breathe with the pump. The song "If I Can Help Somebody" plays. Junior lies there for a while, and Sally walks around.

JUNIOR. I thought I was gone.

The person leaves.

SALLY. You would have if—(*looks around for the person*). That was your guardian angel. Junior, you have been given another chance to get your life together.
JUNIOR. Give me that phone (*he take the phone and dials*). Pastor, this is Junior. Is it too late for you to come over? I do not want to put off any longer. I do believe.

The person is standing in the door and then leaves.

SALLY. The world needs to know there is a danger in putting off. People are stuck in life's ruts because they put off taking steps to change.

Message to reader: Anyone standing on the side of the road, do not put off taking steps to overcome your helpless feeling. Time waits on no one. Set your mind and heart on doing positive things in life by making a difference in the lives of others; and when they laugh, you can laugh. Remember, don't put off trying.

About the Author

Clark Thomas has worked for the state of Arkansas at the Department of Labor Safety division for fifty-two years. For thirty-six years, he has been the project manager for the OSHA consultation program.

He has written several articles and programs on safety topics such as "Speak Up for Safety," "Youth in the Workplace," "Blending Safety and Production," and many others. Clark has made presentations to thousands of workers and CEOs of people relating to safety.

Additionally, Clark is pastor of the New Salem Missionary Baptist Church in rural Arkansas. He has served as pastor for over forty years.

Printed in the USA
CPSIA information can be obtained
at www.ICGtesting.com
LVHW091235210724
786027LV00001B/169